CALEB, THE DEGENERATE

AMS PRESS
NEW YORK

Joseph S. Cotter

CALEB, THE DEGENERATE

A Play in Four Acts

A STUDY OF THE TYPES, CUSTOMS, AND NEEDS OF THE AMERICAN NEGRO

BY

JOSEPH S. COTTER

LOUISVILLE, KENTUCKY
THE BRADLEY & GILBERT COMPANY
1903

Library of Congress Cataloging in Publication Data

Cotter, Joseph Seamon, 1861-
  Caleb, the degenerate.

  1. Negroes--Drama.   I. Title.
PS3505.0862C3 1973   812'.5'2   72-1045
ISBN 0-404-00024-X

Reprinted from the edition of 1903, Louisville
First AMS edition published in 1973
Manufactured in the United States of America

AMS PRESS INC.
NEW YORK, N. Y.   10003

THE AUTHOR

THE AUTHOR is one of a race that has given scarcely anything of literature to the world. His modest tender of some Christmas verses to me led to an inquiry which revealed his story of unpretentious but earnest and conscientious toil. He is wholly self-taught in English literature and composition. The obstacles which he has surmounted were undreamed of by Burns and other sons of song who struggled up from poverty, obscurity, and ignorance to glory.

JOSEPH SEAMON COTTER was born in Nelson County, Kentucky, in 1861, but has spent practically all his life in Louisville. He had the scantiest opportunity for schooling in childhood, though he could read before he was four years old. He was put to work early, and from his eighth to his twenty-fourth year earned his living by the roughest and hardest labor, first in a brick-yard, then in a distillery, and finally as a teamster. At twenty-two his scholarship was so limited that when he entered the first one of Louisville's night schools for colored pupils he had to begin in the primary department. His industry and capacity were so great that at the end of two sessions of five months each he began to teach. He has persevered in his calling, educating himself while at work, and is now Principal of the Colored Ward School at Eighth and Kentucky streets. The man whose advice and encouragement at the beginning chiefly enabled him to accomplish this was Prof. W. T. Peyton, a well-known colored educator of this city, whom he regards as his greatest benefactor.

THOMAS G. WATKINS,
Financial Editor Louisville Courier-Journal.

THE AUTHOR'S PREFACE

THIS play has been in course of construction for some years. Several of the speeches, slightly changed and with suitable headings, have been published in periodicals and in my "Links of Friendship," which will soon be out of print. I once published a short prose version of "CALEB" in a Louisville journal.

Negroes of to-day do not speak in blank verse. The peoples of the past did not. An author puts poetry into the mouths of his characters to show the possibility of individual human expression as illustrated by himself.

The aim is to give a dramatic picture of the Negro as he is to-day. The brain and soul of the Negro are rising rapidly. On the other hand, there is more depravity among a certain class of Negroes than ever before. This is not due to anything innate. It is the result of unwise, depraved leadership and conditions growing out of it.

RAHAB represents this unwise, depraved leadership. CALEB is his pupil, and represents the depraved class of Negroes referred to. Some may claim that the picture is overdrawn, but both leader and led are with us to-day and speak for themselves.

The BISHOP and OLIVIA represent the highest types of cultivated Negro manhood and womanhood. The DUDE represents the so-called educated young Negro politician, of whom something may be made if the right steps are taken in time.

The Negro needs very little politics, much industrial training, and a dogged settledness as far as going to Africa is concerned. To this should be added clean, intelligent fireside leadership. Much of any other kind is dangerous for the present.

I am a Negro and speak from experience.

JOSEPH S. COTTER.

To My Friends

THOMAS J. BROWN

FRANK L. WILLIAMS

LELAND M. FISHER

CHARACTERS.

(All are American Negroes.)

THE BISHOP—Adopted father to Olivia.

NOAH—Father to Olivia.

CALEB—Son to Patsy and Grandison.

GRANDISON.

RAHAB—A minister, politician, and teacher to Caleb.

UNDERTAKER.

DOCTOR.

HIRED MAN.

DUDE.

OLIVIA.

FRONY—Friend to Olivia.

PATSY.

A WAIF.

A WOMAN.

Neighbors, Ministers, Officers, Candidates for Africa, Medical Students, Boys and Girls of Industrial School.

CALEB, THE DEGENERATE.

ACT I.

SCENE I.—Hall in the Bishop's House.

Enter OLIVIA, *playing a violin. The* BISHOP *follows quickly and seizes the bow.*

BISHOP—Reflect, my child, reflect! You should not wed
This Caleb, this hell-builder upon earth.
You counsel well when others are in need.
Yourself you counsel not, or in such wise
Your steps are led not heavenward. No! No!
At times your thoughts have made mine error-proof.
Your views, thrice wedded to occasion, raise
The neighborhood above its ancient self.
Yourself you counsel not. My child, reflect!
[*She begins to play, but stops when he goes on.*]
My darling Margaret is still in mind.
That night! That night! 'T is day, but here it is.
The rain, the thunder, and the lightning's flash,
The twisted timbers and the flooded streams,
The cattle's lowing and the horses' neigh,
Come back to me. I stand beside her bed,
My Margaret's bed. The storm disturbs me not;
For Margaret, my darling Margaret,
Is eying me and whispering my name.
She shall be mine again! Disease's hold
Is lessening. She shall be mine again!
Strength comes! She rises, staggers to the door;
And, ere I am aware of what she means,
Darts out into the storm. I follow her!
"My Margaret! My Margaret!" I cry.
"Health! Health! I go to health!" she answers me.
I can not see. I feel my way about.
The lightning's angry flashing shows her form.
"My Margaret! My Margaret!" I cry.
"'T is health! 'T is health!" cries back my Margaret.
I blunder on and on. The day has come,

And dead and mangled lies my Margaret.
I have one more. 'T is you, Olivia!
You wed a brute, my child?
OLIVIA—   Caleb's the man!
                [*Exit, playing softly.*]
BISHOP—My child, come back! Storms! Lightning! Plague! Come
 back!
   Better be dead with these—Come back! Come back!—
   Than living death with Caleb! Child, come back!
OLIVIA—(*Without.*) What profits it? A child is never grown.
                [*She breaks˙chord on violin.*]
   A broken chord! Chords break so easily.
                Enter FRONY.
BISHOP—Frony!
FRONY—   You have the news?
BISHOP—   Frony, what news?
FRONY—Rahab and Caleb met two nights ago.
BISHOP—The Devil's peace-making is God's despair.
   Rahab was preaching nonsense, was he not?
FRONY—He dealt in facts and logic, strange to say.
BISHOP—His prayers?
FRONY—   His prayers! They change with changeless things.
BISHOP—He prays them full; then kills them with amen.
   He preached in praise of Caleb's evil deeds?
FRONY—He rated him at what he's really worth.
BISHOP—As enemies they hold each other now.
   I took it that the meeting made them friends.
FRONY—It did.
BISHOP—   You may explain. I wait to learn.
FRONY—"You are my subject, Caleb!" Rahab said.
   "I see you sailing, sailing, sailing round
   Perdition—begging, begging to be damned!
   Tarry no longer! Hear the preached word!
   Tarry no longer, lest the brink be passed!
   Be saved! Be saved! Polluted man, be saved!"
BISHOP—Friends after that?
FRONY—   Listen! Some more remains!
BISHOP—(*He hears violin.*) (*Aside.*) I listen! Child! My child!
                [*Music stops.*]
   Go on! I hear!
FRONY—"Be saved?" asked Caleb. "Let us both be saved.
   You drunkard, gambler, hidden libertine!"
   A look! Three steps! A clinch! A fall! A groan!
   Caleb was victor! Rahab raised him up,
   Grasped Caleb's hand and said: "We must be friends!"
BISHOP—'T is strange!
FRONY—   'T is true!
BISHOP—   The end of it?
FRONY—   Murder!

BISHOP—Which killed the other?
FRONY—   Caleb—
BISHOP—   A murderer?
FRONY—What else? A saint?
BISHOP—   This Rahab lived too long.
FRONY—You understand?
BISHOP—   I do!
FRONY—   Rahab's alive.
BISHOP—I do not understand. Explain! Explain!
FRONY—Grandison's dead!
BISHOP—   A horse's kick, or bite?
    I often cautioned him of silly risks.
FRONY—You understand?
BISHOP—   Do I?
FRONY—   'Twas Caleb's hand
    That slew his father.
BISHOP—   Daughter! Daughter! Come!
    Caleb's a parricide! Come! Come! Come! Come!
                    Re-enter OLIVIA.
OLIVIA—Caleb's the man, Bishop!
BISHOP—   He is the—the—
    (*To* FRONY.) You saw. Tell how it was.
FRONY—   His course was wrong.
BISHOP—His father chided?
OLIVIA—   Fathers love to chide!
BISHOP—Give us the full of it! (*To* OLIVIA.) Listen! Profit!
FRONY—Sharp words! Hard blows! A dead man's stare to heaven!
    [BISHOP *breathes hard, staggers and starts to go.*]
OLIVIA—Bishop! [*She looks pale and staggers toward him.*]
FRONY—   Olivia! [*Takes hold of* OLIVIA.]
BISHOP—(*In a rage.*) Caleb's the man!
FRONY—Your daughter, sir!
BISHOP—(*Pathetically.*) My daughter is in love!
    She needs no father.
OLIVIA—(*She starts to him.*) Bishop!
BISHOP—(*Holds hand to heart.*)   Parricide!
    I go! Your father may return with me.   [*Exit slowly.*]
FRONY—To see how woman's wit can cudgel man's?
    (*To* OLIVIA.) The Bishop's wrath—
OLIVIA—   The Bishop's wrath is his.
FRONY—This Caleb is—
OLIVIA—   Not here to damn you back.
FRONY—Is this a case of love?
OLIVIA—   How worketh love?
FRONY—I know it well, and know it not at all.
OLIVIA—Let each explain the other's ignorance.
FRONY—It were a nobler task than wedding brutes.
OLIVIA—A woman you?

FRONY—(*Surprised.*)   Why, yes!

OLIVIA—   Have loved a man?

FRONY—Well—yes!   [*This reservedly.*]

OLIVIA—   Have had an only son?

FRONY—(*Sorrowfully.*)   Yes! yes!

(*Re-enter* BISHOP *with* NOAH, *unseen.*)

OLIVIA—How many women may undo one's son?

FRONY—Mine was so marred by one and dragged to death.

OLIVIA—One kills his body!   Two may save his soul!
    Patsy and I—

FRONY—   Advance you on defeat!

[*On seeing the* BISHOP *and* NOAH *they examine and measure their hands.*]

NOAH—I see.

BISHOP—   What now?

NOAH—   A word perchance—

BISHOP—(*Faint heartedly.*)   Perchance
    A word.

NOAH—   Occasion's ripe.

BISHOP—   Not for success.

NOAH—See you clearly?

BISHOP—   Clearly enough.   Know you
    I 've dealt with women!

NOAH—   Think you more than I?

BISHOP—The case is ours.   You may conduct affairs.

NOAH—Go on!   Go on!

BISHOP—   My way?

NOAH—   Well—yes—your way.

OLIVIA—The way of hands—well—yes—the way of hands—

FRONY—Go on!   Go on!   We 'll measure them again.

[FRONY *measures her own hands and then compares her foot with* OLIVIA'S.
    OLIVIA *looks at* BISHOP.]

BISHOP—I 'll see this Caleb in his mother's house.

NOAH—You 'll see a buzzard wooing God's elect;
    A serpent strangling love and fanging peace.

BISHOP—'T will be an argument that I can use.
    On now to Patsy's.   Grandison lies dead.
    We 'll soothe the mother while we watch the son.

NOAH—The plan is good.   Let 's hasten.   Come you on.

[*He goes out quickly and motions the* BISHOP *to follow.* OLIVIA *has been
    watching the* BISHOP *earnestly.   She looks down and sees* FRONY *com-
    paring their feet.* FRONY *touches* OLIVIA'S *foot with hers.*]

FRONY—A healthy foot!   Mine 's smaller.   Think you so?

OLIVIA—Unfair, Frony!   Ours is a game of hands.

[*The* BISHOP *bows as he calls their names.   They bow in return.*]

BISHOP—Frony!

FRONY—   Bishop!

BISHOP—   Olivia!

OLIVIA—   Bishop!

[*The* BISHOP *goes out slowly, bowing to one and then to the other.*]

FRONY—(*Sarcastically.*) Lover! Buzzard! Serpent! Caleb's the
    man?
OLIVIA—A woman loves—
FRONY—   A buzzard?
OLIVIA—   May be so.
            [FRONY *snaps her fingers.*]
    Caleb's the man! All things combine to show
    His viciousness and prove that he is low.
    Caleb's the man! The world's experience
    Says: "Trust no man who throttles innocence!"
                       [*Exit* FRONY.]

Curtain rises on the next scene as OLIVIA *goes out.*

SCENE II.—A Room in Patsy's Cottage.

ONE DOOR LEADS TO YARD FROM END OF ROOM. AT OTHER END STEPS LEAD
    TO ROOM WHERE GRANDISON LIES DEAD. IN REAR IS A LONG,
    HIGH WINDOW. TWO CHAIRS AND TABLE ARE IN
    ROOM. POVERTY IS STAMPED ON ALL.

Enter RAHAB *from death-chamber. He is followed closely by* FRONY.
PATSY'S *groans come from room. He walks around room, turns
pages of Bible for text.* FRONY *follows and looks over his shoulder.*

RAHAB—Grandison's death is no ill-wind to me.
    I'll preach his funeral. 'T will open ways
    Whereby I may regain a step or two.
    Here is a text that suits the subject well.
             [*He reads aloud.*]
    " Man born of woman is of few days and—"
FRONY—A skunk like you should preach no funeral.
RAHAB—Why? Why? I am a minister! Now, why?
FRONY—You are a scamp, a thief, a devil! a —!
[NOAH *and the* BISHOP *enter hurriedly from yard.* RAHAB, *seeing the*
BISHOP, *runs to chair, sits and turns up coat-collar to hide his face.*]
BISHOP—Frony, we come! Does Patsy bear it well?
FRONY—She does! She groans! She swoons! She is nigh death!
[FRONY *leads them toward death-chamber. The* BISHOP *stops on steps
    and looks at* RAHAB, *whose face is still hidden.*]
BISHOP—That man?
FRONY—   Rahab!
NOAH—   'T is Caleb's devil's man!
[*They enter death-chamber.* PATSY'S *groans are heard. When the
door is slammed,* RAHAB *springs up as from a trap and runs to middle
of floor. He shouts half-circularly. He puffs like a little steam engine
the while. At end he stretches himself and breathes hard.*]

RAHAB—I move me thus, when I am glad at heart.
Who would I be? Myself—my own sweet self!
[*He opens Bible and sits at table.* CALEB *enters from yard unseen, with whip and spurs in hand.*]
Now, to this goodly text. The sermon will—
CALEB—There is no need of sermon.
RAHAB—(*Startled.*)   Think you not?
CALEB—No sermon!
RAHAB—(*He rises.*) Why?
CALEB—(*Moves about.*) Money! Money! Money!
[*He goes to window and calls hired man.*]
You, there! Your laziness is wanted here!
RAHAB—(*He slams Bible on table.*)
(*Aside.*) Worthless! Worthless! I've missed my chance in life!
[*Hired man comes to window.*]
CALEB—(*Gives him spurs.*) Here take my spurs and stick yourself
with them!
[*Hired man stands at window and looks at spurs.* CALEB *goes to door and calls the hired man.*]
You, there! Your laziness is wanted here!
RAHAB—(*To* CALEB.) You are a trainer!
CALEB—   I?
H. MAN—(*At door. Hands spurs to* CALEB.) Your spurs?
CALEB—(*Shoves whip into hired man's face.*)   My whip!
Be off! Your laziness needs stirring up! [*Hired man goes.*]
RAHAB—Your spurs are fine! Your whip is good enough
To flog a fellow such as you had here.
CALEB—The law is all that saves his scaly back.
RAHAB—What need have you for whip and spurs?
CALEB—   My horse!
RAHAB—Your horse?
CALEB—   My horse must clip it! Flesh is naught!
A little breeding serves a righteous end.
RAHAB—You have money! Explain! I am your friend.
CALEB—(*Points to death-chamber.*) Five hundred dollars were upon
his life.
[*Door of chamber is opened.* PATSY *groans.* FRONY *rushes out.* NOAH *stands on steps.* BISHOP *stands in door.*]
FRONY—(*As she rushes out.*) Camphor!
NOAH—(*On steps.*)   Camphor!
BISHOP—(*In door.*)   Camphor!
FRONY—(*Hands bottle to* NOAH.)   Here!
NOAH—(*Hands bottle to* BISHOP.)   Here!
[NOAH *and* BISHOP *rush in.* FRONY *rushes to door and turns to* CALEB *and* RAHAB.]
FRONY—(*Scornfully.*)   Devils!
[*She enters.*]

RAHAB—Five hundred dollars?
CALEB—   Yes, I have it all
Save a few dimes, and they will come ere long.

RAHAB—You've bought him?
CALEB— Yes! Money flies!
RAHAB—(*Makes motion raking in money.*) Meward fly!
You said you'd buy no horse without a tale.
CALEB—He has a tale about him that's a tale.
RAHAB—Tell it!
[NOAH *in door of death-chamber.*]
NOAH—(*To* CALEB.) Your mother swoons!
CALEB—(*To* NOAH.) I tell a tale!
NOAH—Come! Come!
CALEB—(*To* NOAH.) Remain and hear the tale! 'T is smart!
[NOAH *goes in quickly.*]
RAHAB—His cost?
CALEB— I thought you wished the tale.
RAHAB— The cost!
CALEB—He cost a quacking duck and a torn apron.
RAHAB—The tale! The tale!
CALEB—Jasper, the shoemaker, would not be a hatter lest his handi-work treat heads to a sweat, which treats eyes to a smarting, which fills the mind with hard thoughts, which sharpen as they leave the tongue. He would not be a glover lest there be more clapping than wearing. To wear is to prove greatness. To clap is to hand-bawl! A bawler! A bawler! Jasper would not be a bawler! He was—
RAHAB—A shoemaker! Go on with the tale!
CALEB—He was too humane to kill a chinch which circled his neck time and again and ended on the tip of his nose before the whole congregation.
RAHAB—Neither you nor I can understand such humanity. The tale!
CALEB—He was too honest to drink water in which the king's shoe-pegs had been soaked lest he thrive on stolen substance.
RAHAB—The King should have thriven on his blood!
CALEB—Now, Jasper owned a quacking duck that was clock to him in the morning, servant at meal-time, and that feathered his bed at night. A neighbor-woman, who was thirty and nine—and who should have had nine and thirty on her bare back—who talked the neighborhood into confusion, her husband into murder, her sons into theft, and her daughters into ill-marriages, stole the duck and hid it in a barrel.
RAHAB—Woman and mystery always make a good tale. Go on!
CALEB—"Woman," said Jasper, as she was feeding her ducks, "I suspect you of theft!" "Man," said the woman, "I suspect you of insolence! Let's see! Ducky! Ducky! I scatter you honest corn!" "Quack! Quack!" came from the barrel. "There's life in the barrel!" said Jasper. "There's a dream in your head!" replied the woman, and placed her apron over the barrel. "I'll have my duck!" said Jasper, and thrust his hand through the apron and seized the duck. As he held up the apron and duck a stranger rode up on the horse in question. "Fine morning!" said the stranger. "Quack!" Quack!" went the duck. Off! went the horse, leaving the stranger to take his fall as he had it, and his revenge as he could get it. Jasper was affrighted and said: "Who'll own the apron and the duck?" "I own the apron and

the duck!'' said I to the stranger. ''I'll pay the damages!'' said Jasper. ''I'll buy the horse!'' said I. ''Who'll pay for the apron?'' bawled the woman. ''I,'' answered the man and sprang to his feet. Ere I could pay the money the man and woman eloped. They perished in a storm. Jasper buried their bodies by way of damages; and I kept the horse as a matter of business.

RAHAB—A quacking duck and a torn apron! When will a fairy tale be given flesh and blood again?

CALEB—Never! The horse cost me two hundred dollars. I'm feeling gay! When in such moments I am bound to tell a sprightly lie.

BISHOP—(*In door.*)   Your mother is better!

CALEB—(*He frowns.*)   I'm worse!

[*The* BISHOP *shakes his head and goes in.*]

RAHAB—Did you not say the sermon should not be?

CALEB—I did! No sermon! Students will be here!
An undertaker, too! A sham affair!
You understand?

RAHAB—   I do! The sermon's out!

CALEB—I rode the horse to find the students' place.

RAHAB—Your father's horse!

CALEB—   The horse his death-fees bought.
Two hundred dollars of the five! You see?

RAHAB—You are so modern in your filial views.

CALEB—''Weaker and wiser'' is the ancient saw.

[HIRED MAN *appears at the window.* FRONY *enters from death-chamber.*]

FRONY—(*To* CALEB.)   Your mother sleeps!

CALEB—   That sleep will be too short!

HIRED MAN—The undertaker, sir! Five other men!
Four bear a litter!

CALEB—(*To* RAHAB *as he passes out.*)   It will bear the dead!

[*Exit hurriedly to the yard.*]

FRONY—What said he?

RAHAB—   Nothing that amuses you!

FRONY—Beware!

RAHAB—   Of what?   Hell-fire?

FRONY—   You seem to know!

Re-enter CALEB *with* UNDERTAKER.

CALEB—(*To* UNDERTAKER.)   You know your trade?

UNDERTAKER—   I do!

CALEB—(*Points to death-chamber.*)   Make estimate!

[*Exit* CALEB *quickly.* UNDERTAKER *stops and looks around.*]

RAHAB—(*Roughly.*)   That way, death-worm!

FRONY—(*Kindly*)   This way, kind sir!   (*Opens door.*)
Walk in!   (*Enter* UNDERTAKER.   *She closes door.*)
Grandison's blood!

RAHAB—   What know I of his blood?

FRONY—You shed it!

RAHAB—   Caleb shed it!

FRONY—   Your thought helped!

[CALEB *leads five men with a litter past window.* RAHAB *sees.* FRONY
does not.]
You taught him doctrine that will ruin youth.
[*He throws up Bible, catches it and whistles.*]
You sinned so well he loved sin's charming gilt.
RAHAB—I am a master then! Hurrah for me!
Enter CALEB *from death-chamber with* UNDERTAKER.
CALEB—(*To* FRONY.) The doctor enters! Have all come in here!
[FRONY *enters chamber.* CALEB *and* RAHAB *talk aside.* UNDERTAKER
approaches several times to speak, but is waved back by CALEB.]
Enter PATSY. *She groans.*
[*She hobbles in, leaning on* NOAH *and the* BISHOP. *She holds money in
hand.* FRONY *follows and fans her. She is seated. They stand by
her chair.* RAHAB *hugs Bible and looks solemn.*]
CALEB—(*To* UNDERTAKER.) A thirty-dollar coffin? I say no!
Five dollars for a robe? No, death-worm, no!
Four carriages? No, undertaker, no!
Think you a son must curb his appetite
Because a pauper father breathes no more?
The living must have money! I'm alive!
Cold dignity is all the dead require.
The living must have money! Hear you that!
He was my father! I am—well—his heir!
Forgetfulness, I bid you hide the first!
I own the other for its luxury!
Five hundred dollars were upon his life!
I have it all save a few paltry dimes!
(*To* PATSY)—Old woman, you have that? Ah, cigarettes.
[*He takes money from her.*]
Now, undertaker—sober business man!
You see conditions! Make your estimate!
You think about your trade? Drink! Cigarettes!
You'd rob me, sir? Drink! Cocaine! Cigarettes!
I'd stake them, sir, against your trade—your life!
Out! Out! death-worm! Out! Out! You wont? You will!
Offend not living men to serve the dead!
Out! Out! [UNDERTAKER *hurries out.*]
He went! (*To* PATSY)—Old woman, why those tears?
PATSY—(*Faintly.*) Caleb, my boy, where is your heart?
CALEB— Patsy,
Your husband has it in his pauper breast.
He boasted of a hide-bound honesty.
I boast me of my liberty and wit.
BISHOP—(*To* CALEB.) Are you a human being?
CALEB— Look me o'er!
BISHOP—You have a soul?
CALEB— What mean you by that word?
BISHOP—I mean—
CALEB— I would not know your meaning! You

Would make sense senseless in explaining it!
BISHOP—You are a monster!
CALEB— You have spoken truth!
BISHOP—You know not God!
CALEB— You mean God knows not me!
BISHOP—You are an infidel?
CALEB— I am! I am!
BISHOP—You move without a current, sail, or creed!
CALEB—My current is myself! My wit's my sail!
BISHOP—Your creed?
CALEB— I have a creed! It suits you not!
BISHOP—What is it?
CALEB— Here it is! Prepare your ire!
Men stagger in my light, yet are too dull
To see that my creed is infallible.
They rather worship God whose cruel laws
Are made up wholly of mistakes and flaws.
The time shall be when they will cease to follow
Views that are so disgusting and so hollow.
Let blinded Christians, ere they think or stir,
Confer with me, their great philosopher.
When they have steeped their souls in blasphemy,
And trodden under foot theology,
They will be fit to teach true piety.
As I have searched for light should Christians search,
They'll find that faith in God the soul will smirch,
And know that hell's another name for church.
Therefore, my fellow-men, on you I call.
I am your friend, and heartily extol
My creed of life to save you, one and all.
There is my creed!
BISHOP— It is no creed!
CALEB— What then?
BISHOP—'T is soulful nothing with a dash of brain
That sees itself polluted through itself.
FRONY—Our demon!
NOAH— Hell's forerunner!
PATSY—(*Motherly. She rises.*) Caleb—son—
This mother's breast of mine would feed you still!
[STUDENT *taps on window-pane.* CALEB *goes to window.* RAHAB *holds
door leading to yard.* STUDENT *gives* CALEB *money.*]
STUDENT—(*To* CALEB.) Here is your money, sir! We have the corpse!
'T is decomposed a little, but 't will do.
FRONY—Students!
[GRANDISON'S *body is borne by window on a litter.*]
BISHOP—My heavens! Can it be?
FRONY— Students!

PATSY—Caleb, your father! Oh—   [*Falls into* NOAH'S *arms.*]
CALEB—   Be patient, fools!
[BISHOP *peers out window.* FRONY *tries death-chamber door and finds it
    fastened.* CALEB *looks at money and smiles.* RAHAB *motions to him
    to divide.*]

                        Curtain.

                        ACT II.

                SCENE I.—Olivia's Library.

                    Enter OLIVIA.

OLIVIA—'T was horrible! 'T was horrible! Caleb
    Did prove a demon! 'T is my sober thought
    Great God will hear no prayers that he will make.
                Enter FRONY *hurriedly.*
FRONY—You should have seen! You should—
OLIVIA—   I heard enough.
FRONY—Are satisfied?
OLIVIA—   That I should strive the more.
FRONY—I 'd give my life to lead you out of this.
OLIVIA—Lend me your wit. 'T will stand the better watch.
FRONY—Upon which side? Explain! I 'll take a breath!
                [*She sits on chair.*]
OLIVIA—An urchin stretches him upon the ground;
    And, dog-like, laps the water from the spring.
    He fears no ill. He thinks: "I am, therefore,
    I am protected." Life's too full of life
    To shake his faith. So Patsy trusts in God.
    One tells a story till the plot grows dear.
    Men clamor for a change. He says: "Not so!
    I 've put my joys and sorrows into it
    After this fashion." Patsy scorns to change
    Her worship's rule. 'T is life through joy and pain.
    Such constancy is life in league with God.
    She sees no penury in wanting bread
    When that want comes from giving, crumb by crumb,
    One's little store to such as toil for naught.
    A little sock or kerchief or a hood
    Is dearer unto her than volumes filled
    With deeds of men who slay the God in man
    For pen and ink to libel nature with.
    She serves her day by serving her hearth-stone.

FRONY—She is so worthy! Speak the truth of her!
OLIVIA—A button's dropped by some one in a crowd.
One passes it and scarcely sees its form.
Another comes and sees it's what it is,
But goes his way unmindful of its worth.
Another, curious and prudent-wise,
Stores it about him for a future need.
The need may come a score of times, but he
Bethinks him not he has it near at hand.
A wiser one will use it in his need,
Perchance, with others of no kindred. Then
Another, with fine sense of fitness, will
Seek out its fellows somewhere and salute
The seeing eye with wholeness. So we think.
Thoughts face us as we move. We see them not;
Or see them simply recognizably,
And plod along unburdened by their aid;
Or press them to us but ne'er think to use
Such trifles when a serious moment comes;
Or use them in connection where no trace
Of fellowship or kindred may be found.
Few use their thoughts as wisely as a child
Uses the buttons it has found in play.
Patsy is such a thinker. She can think
A thought into the world, and thereby guard
It with the destinies that save the world.
She'll soon give back to earth and air and sky
Her mortal dust, immortal in its trend.
FRONY—She is so worthy!
OLIVIA—   You would help her then?
FRONY—I would!
OLIVIA—   Help me!
FRONY—   To wed—?
OLIVIA—   No argument!
The Bishop comes!
FRONY—   I heard! I know! I'll help!
                        [She rises.]
He would invite you to an argument,
Making this Caleb serve as central point.
He boasts him that if you will listen well
Your thoughts of Caleb shall be spears to prick
Your wild affections into haggardness.
I'll go to meet him! You've a starting point?
His sermons! He is pleased to hear from them.
I like not Caleb, but I'll help you out.
We women must be women! Men are men!   [Exit.]
OLIVIA--I do remember some well-timed remarks
Concerning genius and the fear of hell.

They're from a sermon I once heard him preach.
These will I cite and wed to argument.
I'll at him first! The rule of courtesy
Will steel his patience. (*Steps are heard.*) I do hear his step.
[*Re-enter* FRONY.]
FRONY—Some ministers will seek the Bishop here
 To say good-bye. Can you make use of them?
OLIVIA—I know them well. Each one is practiced well.
 I had it done bethinking of this hour.
 The Bishop?
FRONY—   In his garden!
OLIVIA—   Doing what?
FRONY—Consulting with your father.   [*Exit.*]
OLIVIA—   Plotting still!
 These ministers will play a little part.
 'T will break monotony and give me rest.
 What if the Bishop knew? Appointments? No!
  [*Re-enter* FRONY *with* BISHOP.]
FRONY—You saw this Caleb and remember him.
BISHOP—I did! I do!
FRONY—You think him vile? And thought him worthy of death?
BISHOP—I do! I did!
FRONY—Think you a sermon would be remedy?
BISHOP—No one remembers sermons!
OLIVIA—I do!
FRONY—She does and often speaks to me of yours.
BISHOP—Of mine?
FRONY—Your text, your sermon and your very voice
 She oft repeats to me, and I say true.
 Provoke her, Bishop, and she'll gladly preach
 A part of your own sermon. Try her once!
OLIVIA—As Frony says your sermons cling to me.
BISHOP—As you to Caleb?
OLIVIA—I have no mind to make comparisons.
 Besides the ancient rule of courtesy
 Forbids that you bring up a second point
 When I have introduced a sober first.
BISHOP—'T is true! Go on!
OLIVIA—I heard you preach, and seem to hear you still.
  [*The* BISHOP *takes it for a compliment.*]
 It was on "Genius and the Fear of Hell."
 "The fear of hell doth lift man heavenward."
 This was the gist of half of your discourse.
 I think not so!
FRONY—   I think not so! Bishop,
 You think not so since you have older grown?
 [*The* BISHOP *is silent and buries his head in his hands.*]
OLIVIA—'T would edge my temper and unwing my hope.

FRONY—(*To* BISHOP.) Make that a text and preach the sermon o'er.
[BISHOP *takes Bible from pocket and opens it.*]
OLIVIA—Whenever man is taught the fear of hell,
 He seeks it in the living and the dead.
 See how the ages all do sanction this!
FRONY—You see it, Bishop! Sanction what you see!
OLIVIA—No longer do the airs of Paradise
 Exist for him to hearten and assure.
 No longer does he know that God must still
 O'ermaster Satan ere the soul be dumb.
 Man's ever doomed to woe and death in life,
 To make his faith the tutor to his fear,
 To crush his God and elevate an Imp,
 So long as he does hold such savagery.
 His wild audacity will lead him on
 To smite with slavering hand an angel's face.
 Then straight his witlessness would wonder how
 So pure a stroke could leave so foul a stain.
FRONY—That stroke hit home. Some sparks should be in sight.
OLIVIA—The tragedy of tragedies must be:
 To teach the laws of Heaven so that they cross
 And smite each other till the sons of men
 Know not the voice of God from that of him
 Who sits in Hell, but reigns not anywhere.
FRONY—That is theology. (*To* BISHOP.) Speak I the truth?
[*The* BISHOP *looks through his glasses at the ceiling.*]
OLIVIA—Past ages toyed with man. He knew it not,
 And made their jest the altar of his praise.
 They thorned his soul with fear, yet asked him why
 He was so slow to sniff the Rose of Life.
 They dulled his sight by bringing Hell so close,
 Then scorned him for not seeing Heaven afar.
 The Present should be loath to fellowship
 A Past whose creed made life's sweet peace a dirge.
BISHOP—(*Dryly and slowly.*) Somewhat fatigued, Frony?
FRONY—(*Quickly.*) Are you?
BISHOP—(*Quickly.*)   Are you?
[*He listens attentively.*]
OLIVIA—As some strong man, in firm and joyous mood,
 Plants a small seed beside his cabin door,
 And without thought of fear or future ill,
 Tends it by day and croons o'er it by night
 Until the vine springs up and bears a gourd,
 The which he takes, all famishing of thirst,
 And, step by step, climbs up a shaggy steep
 Where from a stream so small it comes in drops
 He fills it to the brim; but ere he drinks,
 Hears cries from a poor, thirsty traveler

Who pants and groans upon the plain below;
And then, forgetting his own ease and weal,
Bears down the water and so saves a life;
Then as he dies from bruises and of thirst
Thinks all is well since he has humbly served
His gracious Maker in a simple act;
So, you, O, child of Heaven and of Earth,
Must tend your life, making your daily prayer
An ardent wish to gain that you may give;
Feeling no fear, firmly believing that
Nearness to duty, not to burning Hell,
Must ever be the voice that leads to Heaven.

FRONY—Good thought is that! Some seem to think not so.

BISHOP—Duty is ever right. Fear plays its part.
  (*To* OLIVIA.) I spoke of genius. Now, speak you of it.
  What did I say? Do you remember it?

OLIVIA—Yes! You said naught, and I remember it.

FRONY—She told me of it, and I —. (*To* OLIVIA.) Did I laugh?
  Speak on, Olivia!

BISHOP—   Yes! Say your say.
  I worship thought though feminine in garb.

OLIVIA—You lead by questioning. 'T will draw me out.

BISHOP—I question? I?

FRONY—   O, question anything!
  [*Loud coughing without.*]
  Some ministers would say good-bye to you.
  I go to let them in. Now, question on! [*Exit* FRONY.]

BISHOP—I question? I? Let's hear your questioning.

OLIVIA—I'd hear your answering.

BISHOP—   No! No! No! Ask
  You on and on and answer when you will.

OLIVIA—Is genius feminine?

BISHOP—   The question's good.

OLIVIA—Your man of genius is not masculine.
  There's much of woman in him. He prefers
  To keep the secret and the worth of it.
  Is it bred of disease?

BISHOP—   The question's good.

OLIVIA—Eloquence proves not that the vocal chords
  Are in sad plight. So genius and the brain.
  The one who's dull has a diseased brain.
  One's birthright is fine feeling and a true thought
  Is genius satisfied?

BISHOP—   The question's good.

OLIVIA—Rarely, if ever, is it ours to see
  A thinker who is trained harmoniously.
  He who has genius in a certain line
  Allies himself, or may, with the divine.

But mostly is this done at the expense
Of a well-planned and rounded excellence.
The gods proclaim that he is doubly blessed.
He cries: "Begone, ye gods! I am distressed!"
[FRONY shows two ministers in.]
FRONY—*(At door.)* In! In! The Bishop waits. He's in a mood!
[They enter and whisper aside. FRONY goes back.]
Enter NOAH.
NOAH—I'll in myself! What's going to happen here?
BISHOP—Remain and see!
NOAH—*(To BISHOP.)* You've been successful, eh?
FRONY—*(Looks in.)* Remain and see! *[She comes in.]*
NOAH— I will!
BISHOP—*(To NOAH.)* Come to my side. *[He goes.]*
[The ministers stand on either side of table and toss ball to each other.
OLIVIA and FRONY let their hair so fall that it covers back of head
and face. They stand with arms around each other's neck and rock
to and fro.]
OLIVIA—Ball! Ball!
FRONY— That means a little game. Ha! ha!
[They continue to rock and measure first hands and then feet. Ball rolls
under table. Ministers upset table in getting it. BISHOP'S hat falls.
First Minister rubs his head with one hand and hands hat to Second
Minister, who does same and hands hat to NOAH. NOAH takes it
and wipes it reluctantly. Ministers whisper again.]
BISHOP—My hat! Is this a game of ball? My hat!
NOAH—Stay, Bishop, stay! You see just what you see!
BISHOP—I stay! Is this a trick? Then let me learn!
Even a sober man may smile at whims.
FIRST MINISTER—*(Lays ball on table.)* Here, Bishop!
SECOND MINISTER—*(Puts down doll-shoes.)* Here, Bishop!
[Third minister enters hurriedly, lays on table doll-toys and loaf of bread.]
THIRD MINISTER— Bishop, look well!
FRONY—The game! The game!
OLIVIA— Who'll live to see it out?
[First and Second Ministers run to OLIVIA and FRONY and fan them with
their beavers. NOAH puts BISHOP'S beaver on table and goes to door.]
BISHOP—Noah, you go?
NOAH— My wits won't let me stay. *[Exit NOAH.]*
[OLIVIA and FRONY put up their hair.]
BISHOP—Things seem to say: "Be philosophical."
You'd have a game? Let each one take a part.
[First and Second Ministers give their hats to Third Minister to hold.
He bows and holds them with dignity.]
Draw near! *(All draw near.)* OLIVIA, take you the ball!
Good Ministers, take each a little shoe!
The loaf of bread, Frony! *(To THIRD MINISTER.)* Some of
the toys?
THIRD MINISTER—Bishop, I'm toying now with this headwear
That wears so well a score of years might fail

To see its gloss in need of hatter's aid.
Suppose my grandfather had owned these hats;
Suppose they came to me as his estate;
Suppose I brought them to a place like this;
Suppose I fanned two ladies, side by side;
Suppose I gave them to a friend to hold;
Suppose he held them in his sturdy left;   [*Holds them so.*]
Suppose he drew his right and poised it thus;
            [*He draws as though to strike.*]
   Suppose—
MINISTERS—   We take our beavers back again.
    [*They take them and lay them aside.*]
BISHOP—(*To* THIRD MINISTER,)   What would you have?
   We would not slight you, sir.
THIRD MINISTER—(*Walks to* FRONY *and points to bread.*)
   A slight division of the honors here.
OLIVIA—I'll squeeze. (*She squeezes the ball.* FIRST MINISTER *points
   to* SECOND MINISTER'S *feet and to little shoes.*)
FIRST MINISTER—How many pairs will make a pair?
   [FRONY *looks at bread as though she would eat it.*]
FRONY—My teeth are many years younger than I.
THIRD MINISTER—(*Aside.*) I do not ask for a division there.
BISHOP—These trinkets seem to tell a sober tale.
I see a people, friendless, ignorant,
Living from hand to mouth, from jail to grave.
They wander here and there, scorning the moss
That clutches to the heel of industry.
They swarm into the towns with empty heads,
With idle hands that know not handicraft,
With vicious appetites that lead to death,
With views of life a child might scorn to hold.
They know the past but as a burial ground.
No friendly spectre rises up therefrom.
A thousand years of life glare in their face.
They glare again and mock their seriousness.
When God turns politician they are saints.
Philosophy is made to lag behind.
A childish intuition's asked to point
A certain finger toward the times to be.
How poor, how helpless, how misguided they!
MINISTERS—Bishop, these trinkets tell a sober tale.
OLIVIA—(*Aside to* FRONY.) The secret's out! How happened it?
FRONY—   I guess!
OLIVIA—Your guess?
FRONY—(*Aloud.*) The Ministers kept not their word.
MINISTERS—The Bishop makes appointments! That means much!
OLIVIA—Bishop, we would explain the whole affair.
FRONY—It shall be plain.
BISHOP—   Let it come further on!

MINISTERS—The Bishop knows, and he'll explain it well.
BISHOP—These people, my beloved people, must
    Be wise to know, be skilled to seize the shaft
    That sets in motion life's unnumbered wheels.
    The head! The hand! The hand! The head! These two
    Will save the noble remnant. Let us act!
OLIVIA—Let us act!
FRONY—   Let us act now!
MINISTERS—   Let us act!
BISHOP—The ball means progress.
OLIVIA—(*Tries to make the ball bigger.*)   I'll not squeeze it more.
BISHOP—It means the progress that draws after it
    The things we eat and wear and use in life.
FIRST MINISTER—These little shoes are very small. How's that?
BISHOP—The smallness shows how scant our footing is.
    We are a baby that's too small to shoe.
    Ages ago the white man's effort dropped
    A pebble in the sea of progress. Now,
    Circles that gird the universe are seen.
    We drop a pebble in to-day. We see
    Our pebble but the white man's circle. Strange!
FRONY—My teeth are younger far than I, but I
    Can see you see the game we wished to play.
THIRD MINISTER—(*Aside.*)   Each speech is seasoned with her younger
    teeth.
OLIVIA—The bread means what?
BISHOP—   The Bible tells us that
    In our own brow's sweat shall we eat our bread.
FRONY—The doll-toys, Bishop?
BISHOP—   They are models of
    The many things we need to learn to make.
OLIVIA—(*To* MINISTER.)   You told!
FRONY—(*To* MINISTER.)   You told!
FIRST MINISTER—   We did!
SECOND MINISTER—   We did!
BISHOP—   They did!
OLIVIA—We meant to play and then explain the game.
    We train the hand. Our boys and girls find books
    Are good to make, to guide, to let alone.
    Making a book is caging life's best life.
    Go, cage life's life before you pause to read.
    Books guide you when you own their soul and thought.
BISHOP—Industrial training is the thing at last.
FRONY—How dull we were!
OLIVIA—   How far we looked to learn
    A truth that's taught by jingling pots and pans.
MINISTER—(*To* OLIVIA.)   Are we excused?
OLIVIA—   Address the Bishop there!

MINISTERS—Good-by, Bishop!
BISHOP— Frony, they say good-by!
FRONY—I 'll go with them and talk the matter o'er.
THIRD MINISTER—I 'll go with you. The bread is tempting still.
[FRONY *goes out. The* MINISTERS *follow with toys in their beaver hats.*]
Enter NOAH *slowly.*
BISHOP—Well! Well! Noah! Your wits won't let you stay?
[*Exit* NOAH *quickly.*]
[OLIVIA *holds the* BISHOP'S *beaver and motions him to toss the ball. He does. She catches it in hat.*]
OLIVIA—My hat! Is this a game of ball? My hat!
BISHOP—Olivia, my child, it is a game
Of progres that I riddled out for you.
[*She puts hat on table.*]
OLIVIA—To-morrow night at our industrial school
My pupils show their work. Be there on time!
BISHOP—I learned your little game.
OLIVIA— You learned it well.
What think you of the force of handicraft?
BISHOP—God's love and handicraft must save the world.
OLIVIA—You 've seen my book—"The Negro and His Hands?"
BISHOP—I have not read it.
OLIVIA— I will give you one.
[*She goes out to get book.*]
BISHOP—How she evades! Ha! ha! That little game!
That little riddle on industrial work!
She thought to puzzle me and then explain.
The ministers would blab! I did the rest.
She cunningly evades at every point.
Caleb's my theme. Directness wins her scorn.
There am I weak.
Re-enter OLIVIA.
OLIVIA— Somehow I have misplaced
The book. 'T was my last copy.
BISHOP—(*Aside.*) I see now!
You gave the book to Caleb?
OLIVIA— I did not.
BISHOP—'T was in his hands. He said it was your last.
You have one copy of yourself. Beware!
OLIVIA—The rule of courtesy is potent still.
Caleb is not the subject.
[*She looks at books on shelf.*]
BISHOP—(*Aside.*) Books! Books! Books!
[*He looks at books on another shelf, holds one up and reads lead-pencil writing on back. She thinks he reads title.*]
"The Negro and His Hands."—Olivia.
[*She starts to him.*]
OLIVIA—You 've found it? Now, take back your hasty charge.
[*He still holds up book.*]

BISHOP—'T is written plainly with a lead-pencil.
> *[She returns to book-shelf.]*

(*Aside.*) Another indirection, win or lose!
(*To* OLIVIA.) Your ideal man?

OLIVIA— I have him.

BISHOP— Let me hear.

OLIVIA—He is a man who lives a peaceful life
Which kills from a continual round with strife.
His being born without a single fear
Makes him of course an abject coward here.
He grows so fast the growing duly stunts,
And breathes so smoothly that he always grunts.
The more he learns, the more he sees 't is needed
To keep his empty mental-garden weeded.
When men are killed outright and resurrected
He holds such little things should be expected.
And to become, thinks he, extremely wise
One simply has to misapply his eyes.
And seeing things as they will never be
Leads ever on to true philosophy.
By placing twilight at the early dawn
He stops his motion while he still goes on.
Humility in him is two-edged pride,
And what 's in glory is not glorified.
He makes an everlasting truce with death,
Then straightway turns and draws his latest breath.

BISHOP—That character 's impossible. Again!

OLIVIA—His is an eye that runs compassion's length.
His is a tongue that snares the simplest words
Round simplest thoughts in beauty's fadeless mesh.
Such art as his the soul of man endears
Through all the silences of all the years.
Right-fettered and full-faced he halts him by
Each column wrong has builded to the sky.
He flaws each flaw until proof-laden runs
Faith's highest hope past earth and stars and suns.

BISHOP—That is not Caleb—

OLIVIA— Well you know 't is not.

BISHOP—Again!

OLIVIA— How many think you I possess?

BISHOP—Enough to banish Caleb.

OLIVIA— He 's secure.

BISHOP—What think you of his creed—his atheist's creed.
He thundered it into his mother's ears.
He blurted it above his father's corpse.

OLIVIA—I think not of it now. I do not wish.
Accept the creed of strenuous modern life?

BISHOP—Of strenuous modern life? Well, let me hear.

OLIVIA—God makes a man. Conditions make his creed.
When reason's torch has once been kindled by
The vicious fancies of the ignorant
And fueled by the greed and soullessness
That stamp eternal vengeance everywhere,
The human in us often scoffs and says:
"There is no God nor Heaven to be found.
Hope is the star that lights self unto self.
Faith is the hand that clutches self's decree.
Mercy is oil self keeps for its own ills.
Justice is hell made present by a blow.
Conditions, therefore, make this creed I hold:
God-like I strive, but man-like I rebel!"
Man is most man, and, therefore, most like God
When he does weigh life's actions in such scales
As balance not for his sufficiency,
But quiver till the All-intelligence
Applies a power whose name is very truth.
Great men, not creeds, will have the right of way.
BISHOP—(*He calls as to one afar off.*) Caleb! Caleb! You have the
right of way.
A great man, you? (*Takes up his hat.*) Ha! ha! (*Starts
to door.*) Ha! ha! (*Bows to* OLIVIA.) Ha! ha! (*He
raises hat to put it on. Ball falls to floor. He hurries
out. She begins with last line pronounced.*)
OLIVIA—Great men, not creeds, will have the right of way.
They clash in every age; and clashing strip
Some worn-out garment from the limbs of Truth.
Should one put forth his eager hand and touch
Truth's perfect robes they would entangle it
And hold it captive till God's reckoning time.   [*Exit.*]
Curtain.

SCENE II.—Patsy's Orchard.

[*At the rising of the curtain* PATSY *is lying on a couch. Her head is
bandaged and slightly elevated.* CALEB *sits in a chair, nodding and
holding in his mouth a partly-consumed cigarette.* PATSY *claps her
hands to arouse him.*]
PATSY—(*Clapping her hands.*) Caleb, my boy! My breath! My
breath! Caleb!
Come! Come! A kiss! A touch! Caleb! My breath!
[*She tries to clap her hands, but simply beats the air.*]
O, God, forgive my boy! My—breath—is—short. [*She dies.*]
Enter BISHOP *and* FRONY.
[*They go to the bed and examine* PATSY. CALEB *awakes.*]

FRONY—(*To* CALEB *softly.*)   Patsy is dead.
CALEB—(*After lighting his cigarette.*)   She is?   Then bury her.
[*He remains in the chair and smokes with dignity.*   FRONY *arranges bed,*
    crosses PATSY'S *hands and feels her forehead.*]
BISHOP—(*Pointing to bandage.*)   That bandage on your mother's head!
CALEB—   I see!
BISHOP—How came it there?
CALEB—   She fell.
BISHOP—   How happened it?
CALEB—You know?   Then tell.   I do not deal in dreams.
BISHOP—(*Coming closer.*)   You tell me you could listen?
CALEB—   Yes!   Why not?
    'T is but a serious trifle.   Speak!   I hear!
    [BISHOP *steps aside, rubs his hands and looks puzzled.*]
FRONY—(*Points to chair in which* CALEB *sits.*)   'T was in that very
    chair she sat.
CALEB—(*Playfully.*)   And dreamed.
BISHOP—Of you!
CALEB—   You fear to tell a dream?   Then speak!
FRONY—'T was from that chair she fell!
BISHOP—   Her bandaged head!
FRONY—Her death has followed.
BISHOP—   How she did cry out:
    "My baby!   My Caleb!   Perdition!"
CALEB—   Whew!
    You are so easily excited!   Whew!
BISHOP—(*Takes hold of chair.*   CALEB *nods in answer to each question.*)
    'T was in this chair she sat?   From it she fell?
    Her head was cut?   She suffered days and months?
    Her death came from that fall?
CALEB—(*Nods several times.*)   I'll nod and nod!
    Your other questions now are answered.   Whew!
    The dream!
FRONY—   I heard her tell it oft.   I wept
    Each time.
BISHOP—   Who could refrain?
CALEB—   Tell it and see.
BISHOP—After this manner did she speak.
CALEB—(*Lightly.*)   Come on!
BISHOP—" Methought my Caleb was a babe again.
    I pressed his head to mine and crooned and crooned
    A baby ditty—old, nonsensical—
    Yet ever sweet to each true mother's heart.
    When he said ' dad ' I kissed his chin, mouth, nose,
    Eyes, forehead; breathed and kissed them o'er again.
    Five years passed by.   He sat upon my knee
    While I placed roses on his tender brow.
    Ten years passed by.   I saw him stand above
    His school-mates in their studies and their games.

Again I looked and saw a man full-grown—
I, bent and gray, leaning upon his arm—
Loved by the just, respected by the wise.
Swift Time, the robber, beckoned to my babe.
I pinched his chin and kissed it o'er and o'er.
I clapped his hands and kissed until he laughed.
I rubbed his feet and kissed and kissed and kissed.
I fell asleep. When I awoke my babe
Was lying on the floor. Thinking 't was hurt,
I screamed ' my babe.' Straightway it was a man—
Caleb, the heartless. ' Caleb,' then I called.
A flame of fire sprang up. It circled him.
I cried: 'Perdition! Save! O, God! O, God!'
I leaped to help him. O, this head of mine!
'T will be my death! A mother's love is all
Of God's great love and all the million pangs
Of mother-hood can drive into her soul.''

CALEB—I have refrained. Come, Frony, with your tears.

[FRONY *removes bandage from* PATSY'S *head and shows scar across forehead.*]

FRONY—This scar will place the word ingratitude
    'Cross Heaven's gate. Your doom—
CALEB—   To hear tame speech.
BISHOP—Your mother told this dream. You heard! You scoffed!
    You came one morning, hungry, barefooted.
    " Shoes, Patsy! Money, Patsy!" This you said.
    She leaned to kiss you and—
CALEB—   I shoved her off.
    That scar is ugly. My fine taste rebelled.
BISHOP—She saw your feet. She thought of how she kissed
    Them in her dream. She stooped—
CALEB—   I coldly said:
    " 'T is not caresses. It is shoes I want."
BISHOP—You got them?
CALEB—   Yes! It was her place to give.
        [FRONY *looks upon* PATSY.]
FRONY—Her eye-lids quiver! She's alive—alive!
    Patsy's alive!
      [BISHOP *runs to bed.* CALEB *is undisturbed.*]
BISHOP—   Let's see! No! No! She's gone!
CALEB—You are so easily excited. Whew!
BISHOP—You slew your father. Now, I understand.
    You have all God condemns the Devil for.
CALEB—Sink not good manners in fine eloquence.
BISHOP—Look on your father through your mind's eye.
CALEB—   No!
    He's gone! Let him continue! Speak! I sleep!
    [*He pretends to sleep. He snores.*]

BISHOP—You turn yourself into a spurious coin
          And boast that it has naught that recommends.
          Bad, worse, worst, worsted you! Naught can come next!
[*He snores more loudly. The* BISHOP *shakes him roughly.*]
          You sleep? The slaying of your father wins
          A blissful rest? You sleep? Defaming her
          Who gave you life—
                    [CALEB *tries to rise.*]
CALEB—   Let me confess!
BISHOP—   Is just?
          You sleep?
CALEB—(*On his feet.*) I would confess!
BISHOP—(*Forcing him to his knees.*) No! No! Sleep on!
CALEB—I will confess! I 'd wed your foster-child!
BISHOP—You 'd wed? I 'd slay! [*Throws him to ground. Lifts his
          foot to stamp him in face.*] I 'd slay! [*Lowers his foot.*]
          Oh, I forgot!
          Your mother 's dead, and I 'm a man of God.
[*He kneels at* CALEB'S *side in attitude of prayer.* CALEB *groans.* FRONY
looks into PATSY'S *face. Curtain falls. It rises immediately.* CALEB
stands aside and looks dignified. The BISHOP *still kneels and looks
toward Heaven. Many neighbors have come to see* PATSY. *As* OLIVIA
enters CALEB *looks abashed and runs out. The curtain falls. It
rises immediately on next scene.*]

SCENE III.—Patsy's Orchard.

Enter NOAH, *chased in by* CALEB.
CALEB—(*Yells in* NOAH'S *ear.*) Hello, graybeard! Would have good
          company?
          Have mine and answer as I question you.
          Olivia and I— You see the point?
          Too dull to see? You need a shaking up!   [*Shakes him.*]
          Olivia and I would— (NOAH *shows disgust.*) How you frown!
          It pleases me. Ho, blessed privilege!
          Olivia and I would wed.
NOAH—(*Scornfully.*)   No! No!
CALEB—You say no, no! I say yes, yes, Graybeard!
          You need a son-in-law. Now, listen well!
          I am a gambling man. Have heard of it?
          Have not? You should know all my noble parts.
          Confusion halts for me. Peace hastens by.
          God I reject. Woman I may accept.
          Graybeard, you need a son-in-law like me.
          I prophesy for you. Now, listen well!

A thief you'll be. [*Makes movements of picking chickens.*]
Chickens! chickens! chickens!
You've stolen one. You have it in the pot.
Your thumb and finger grip a steaming leg.
Some of the meat is sizzling in your mouth.
A voice without says: "Noah, let me in.
I fear my chicken's feeding in your coop."
"No! no!" you say, and take another bite.
The voice goes on without, and you within.
You need a son-in-law to prophesy.
I see you sitting there beside a post.
Soap, water, brushes, combs are set aside.
Your color's that of dirt. Your lice are fat.
They and your finger nails have scabbed your back.
What's in your hand? A pair of ancient dice.
You shake them thus and thus. [*Makes motion of shaking.*]
You throw them thus. [*Makes motion of throwing.*]
You frown and curse. You rub your back and smile.
No fellow-player? Money is at stake?
No! No! Graybeard! You gamble with yourself,
Or rather with the lice upon your back.
They bite a hundred places all at once.
You'd season pain with fun. Therefore, you cast
The dice to see where first to make attack.
[NOAH *starts to leave.* CALEB *leads him back by his beard.*]
I'll tell you when to shun a bit of truth.
[NOAH *leans against a tree and trembles.*]
You need my sense. I prophesy again.
Drunk! drunk! Graybeard? 'Tis a most natural thing.
Drunk! Drunk! You sit beside an ancient fire.
The back-log sputters. You reply to it:
"I'll be with you when you do come to me."
I laugh and take you for my cuspidor.
The back-log sputters. You say: "Wait a bit,
Or come my way. I am a sober man,
A gentleman who never— Drinks you say?
Three full ones, if you please! I come! I come!"
You jump behind the log. I laugh and spit.
You are a crackling now. I say amen.
You need a son-in-law. Olivia
And I would wed. What think you of the match?
[NOAH *starts to go.* CALEB *holds him by the beard.*]
Answer!

NOAH—   I go to bury Patsy.
CALEB—   I
Would wed Olivia. The exchange is fair.
Your beard is long enough. A little pull
Will give you speech. [*Pulls it.*]
NOAH—   My beard!

CALEB—   Answer, I say!

NOAH—I go to dig your mother's grave.

CALEB—   You must
Remain awhile to please that mother's son.

NOAH—She must be buried.

CALEB—   I must have a wife.
[*Pulls out beard and throws it down.*]

NOAH—My beard is being wasted.

CALEB—   What of that?
My strength is not.

NOAH—   Oh! Oh!

CALEB—   Ha! Ha! Answer!

NOAH—Ye-es.

CALEB—(*Mimics.*) Ye-es!   [*Evens up beard with knife.*]
You are adorned.   Your son-in-law
Would thank you, but he has not heart enough.
[*Exit* CALEB.]

[NOAH *picks up scattered beard and puts it into pocket-book.   He looks
for more beard as* BISHOP *enters.*]

Enter BISHOP *unseen.*

NOAH—(*On all-fours looking for beard.*)   Olivia!

BISHOP—(*Softly, beckoning.*)   Olivia!

NOAH—   Quickly!

Enter OLIVIA.

BISHOP—Quickly! (*Points to* NOAH.)   A mystery I can not solve!
[*Exit* BISHOP.]

OLIVIA—A mystery this is I fain would solve.
Father!

NOAH—   O, loss! O, precious loss!

OLIVIA—(*Takes hold of him.*)   Rise! Rise!

NOAH—(*Pulls back.*)   I'm nearer to my loss.

OLIVIA—   What is the loss?

NOAH—Who wrought it better ask.

OLIVIA—   Please tell it me!

NOAH—(*Rises.*)   I would acquaint you of my morning's work.
I take a hand in Patsy's burial.
[*He kisses her three times.*]
The first is for your mother who was wise.

OLIVIA—In wedding you?   I never heard her say
So much when she did curtain lecture you.
You should have said my mother who was brave.

NOAH—That's lightly said.

OLIVIA—   Its truth has weight enough.

NOAH—The second, child, is for your innocence. [*Kisses her again.*]
The third—the third—

OLIVIA—   Is what? Now, let me hear.

NOAH—It is my dying kiss—my curse! Go! Go!

OLIVIA—That extra kiss? I see! It would commend—

NOAH—This Caleb to the jaws of hungry dogs.

OLIVIA—Your views are human—
NOAH— When my foes are less.
Go!
OLIVIA— I go not alone. No parting kiss?
None? I go not alone.
NOAH— Alone? No! No!
The woes of earth condensed will be your guide.
Re-enter BISHOP.
Go! Go!
BISHOP— Wait yet awhile.
NOAH— Go! Go!
BISHOP— Wait yet.
NOAH—You compromise!
BISHOP— You speak unwittingly!
Her views are wrong, but who does not applaud
A will like hers that brooks no veering wind?
A brain that blots out custom's diary?
NOAH—Good sense applauds the workings of good sense.
Call nonsense what you please. I take my leave.
[*Opens pocket-book and looks at beard as he goes out.*]
BISHOP—Your way is yours, and you will see it through.
Now, tell me plainly why you take this course.
'T is not a case of love?
OLIVIA— What think you, sir? [*Exit* OLIVIA.]
Curtain.

ACT III.

SCENE — Working-Room of Industrial School.

[*On one side are anvil, hammer, forge, benches for shoemakers and carpenters. On the other are tables and chairs for sewing-girls. Rocking-chair, desk, and other things made by carpenters are on exhibition. Walls are lined with work by blacksmiths, shoemakers, and sewing-girls. A screen stands off aside. A small blackboard hangs on rear wall. There is empty space on wall where horse-shoes are to be hung. Boys and girls are uniformed. On the rising of the curtain the* BISHOP *stands alone. He strikes the anvil with a hammer and lays it aside.*]

BISHOP—That sound is the password to Negro enfranchisement. Muscle woos the field. Brain woos the market. Wedded they conquer the world. He, in whom they unite, may issue the contract for running all things and award it to himself.

[*Enter* OLIVIA *examining a piece of sewing. The* BISHOP *follows her and tries to steal a kiss.*]

OLIVIA—(*Turning.*) As many as you wish, Bishop-father.

BISHOP—(*Kisses her.*) Some boys came to steal my roses. I tapped upon the window-pane and frightened them away. They came again. Again I tapped. Again they fled. I bethought me of some such trick my boyhood's follies knew. I said: "Come, boys! Roses, boys! Have your fill!" Said one: "Thanks, sir! If we can't have the pleasure of stealing your roses, we don't want them." My dear Olivia, 'tis sometimes so with kisses.

OLIVIA—You are not all theologian. You are part man.

BISHOP—The boys and girls?

OLIVIA—They will enter soon.

BISHOP—How pass the time?

OLIVIA—Speech-making!

BISHOP—The speaker?

OLIVIA—You!

BISHOP—The subject?

OLIVIA—Let the occasion suggest. Look! Real anvil, real shoes, real everything!

BISHOP—Real work!

OLIVIA—Yes!

BISHOP—Real life then!

OLIVIA—Yes! How tardy it is!

BISHOP—How unreal has been the Negro's past! We are a primitive people.

OLIVIA—Very!

BISHOP—With civilized ideas.

OLIVIA—That are mostly borrowed.

BISHOP—What a damning combination!

OLIVIA—Why, Bishop! You speak truthfully though.

BISHOP—'Tis like a monkey among clocks and watches. The clocks seem to say: "Stop!" The watches say: "Go on!" The watches are hurled at the clocks, and both are ruined. When silence reigns, the monkey says: "I have set progress a foot." 'Tis a damning combination.

OLIVIA—Emphasize it, Bishop.

BISHOP—Many a naked African is superior to the Negro American collegian. His simple thought is his own, and he can give it an original setting. Witness the proverbs and fables among the wild Africans. Witness the vast amount of undigested thought in the other case.

[*Enter four girls who examine tools and other things on boys' side.*]

OLIVIA—How make the Negro more original?

BISHOP—He must follow the laws of inquisitiveness and necessity. Till then he is a puppet where there is no material for laughter, and is straightway silenced out of court.

OLIVIA—Give an example.

BISHOP—I am alone. I see the heavens, the earth, and a wild boar. The boar would pierce me, but I seize a rock and break off its tusks. When hungry I slay the boar and eat. As I lie upon the ground old age creeps through me. I arise and build me a house in the boughs of the trees. As I look down upon the damp earth and the bones of the boar I see what lessons I have learned from necessity. As I look from my house and behold the moon, stars, and blue expanse above I grow inquisitive. Gratitude and inquisitiveness wed, and from them I spring a child of song to sing and sing of what I have seen and felt.

OLIVIA—How cultivate his own style?

BISHOP—His thought must spring from action, and his words from sheer necessity. He who has a thought has a style. Start a handful of snow down a hill. At the foot it is a huge ball. Thus thought finds words for its utterance.

OLIVIA—Give an example of thought and style.

BISHOP—A dog attacks a cat. The cat claws not, bites not. It simply humps its back, and the dog retires.

OLIVIA—What will you draw from that?

BISHOP—A proverb showing thought and style.

OLIVIA—Give it.

BISHOP—The hump in the back, rather than the sharpness of the claws, protects the cat.

OLIVIA—One more!

BISHOP—A person with rheumatism is undignified in movements.

OLIVIA—Now, for that.

BISHOP—Few cultivate dignity and rheumatism at the same time.

OLIVIA—The Negro would be literary.

BISHOP—He would. Let him put his brain into his muscle and both into the world around him, and he will be.

OLIVIA—Industrial training makes—

BISHOP—For health, wealth, morals, literature, civilization.

[Two girls lift a hammer with difficulty and strike an anvil. The others stand by and go through same motions. When hammer strikes all breathe hard. They stop and rub each other's arms. BISHOP examines rocking-chair. Boys and girls enter with tools. OLIVIA directs them to places. Blacksmiths, carpenters, and shoemakers take their places. Girls go to their side for sewing. Boy and girl stand aside with pencils and pads. All hold up tools and stand ready to begin work.]

Congratulations, boys and girls! Again
Congratulations! This is life—real life.
The brow's pure sweat has kept the world God-like.
A hatchet, saw, or hammer in your hand
Is far more eloquent than learned words,
If there be skill to use, spirit to dare.
Each man unto his sphere. The laws of God
Will have it so. Agree with law and live.
Sloth marshalled yesterday to destiny,
A destiny that makes to-day a death,
A death that's resurrected by the clang
Of tools in brawny hands, of energy,
Thought-pointed, in the markets of the world.
Agree with law and live. You have been told
A silver tongue can steer a nation's bark.

Look at the idle prattle of the past.
Unreal has been our life. We sought with straws
To leverage what others did with steel.
We turned our hopes to bubbles, proudly blew
And wondered why they sent no answer back.
Agree with law and live. 'T is yours to send
A thrill progressive through the race's heart.
'T is yours to realize God's ancient way
Of taming savagery through handicrafts.
Let clang the anvil!   [*Blacksmith strikes shoe.*]
            Let the saw's sharp teeth
Gnaw passways through and through rebellious wood.
            [*Carpenters begin to saw.*]
Progress can not outstrip the needle's point,
Therefore, your needles, girls—your needles, girls.
            [*Girls begin to sew.*]
Attend, my boys—you of the awl and pegs.
Be clear of sight! Cut straight! Sew well! Know that
Man is but little better than his shoes.
[*Shoemakers begin to work. All are ready to begin.*]
            Ready?
ALL—   Ready!
BISHOP—   To earn your bread?
ALL—   Aye! Aye!
BISHOP—To do the right?
ALL—   Always!
BISHOP—   To help mankind?
ALL—'Till life shall end!
BISHOP—   Let go! You lead the race!

[*All work vigorously. Enter* FRONY *and* WOMAN *with* OLIVIA'S *book.
They sit back to back and search books. Boy and girl with pencils
and pads watch workers and write compositions.* BISHOP *and* OLIVIA
*move about and examine work. Boys hold up work and examine it.
Girls sew on.* OLIVIA *directs them.*]

FRONY—(*To* WOMAN.) What seek you?
WOMAN—   What seek you?
FRONY—   A laugh!
WOMAN—   Find it!
            [*They search books.*]
BISHOP—(*To* BOY *and* GIRL.) I' ll read your compositions, little ones.
BOY—Mine first!
GIRL—   Mine first!
BISHOP—   Both first. Each sentence shall
            Draw from both compositions.
GIRL—(*Points to* BOY.)   His thoughts!
BOY—(*Points to* GIRL.)   Her words!
BISHOP—What shall the gender of the sentence be?
BOY—Don't know. I 'll think.
GIRL—   Don't know. I 'll pray not to.

FRONY—Ha! ha!

WOMAN—   You found the laugh? Where? Where?

FRONY—   Nowhere!

    I laughed to cheer me up to find the laugh.

WOMAN—You might have made me laugh a real laugh.

GIRL—Do laugh!

BOY—   A real laugh!

GIRL—   'T will bring again

    The bloom—[FRONY *and* WOMAN *spring from their seats and
        face each other.*]

FRONY AND WOMAN—(*Pointing to each other.*)   You lost some twenty
    years ago.   [*Boys resume their work quietly.*]

OLIVIA—That ring is better than the ring of words.

        [*Girls hold up work and examine it.*]

FRONY—(*Holds up book.*)   The laugh is here.

WOMAN—   How know you that?

FRONY—   The book

    Was written by Olivia.

WOMAN—(*Holds up book and strikes it.*)   'T is here.

[*Woman sits and nods.* FRONY *consults* OLIVIA *about book.* BISHOP
    reads children's composition.]

BISHOP—"They sew my heart into the fabrics there."

GIRL—My words! Your thoughts! 'T is masculine!

BOY—   No! no!

BISHOP—"He thrones my heart upon the anvil there."

BOY—Your words! Your thought! It is so feminine.

GIRL—How read you that?

BOY—   'T is what I wish to know.

BISHOP—Explain it to yourselves some far on day
    When you have lived and learned. [BISHOP *sits in chair and
    rocks.*]

BOY—   And we have wed.

    [*Girl covers her face with pad.*]

GIRL—Go shame yourself for speaking as you feel.

BOY—Go think of it and shame me with consent.

[WOMAN *drops book, laughs and runs out. Girls laugh. Boys keep time
working with their tools. Boy and girl strike heads together. Enter*
RAHAB *and* DUDE, *magnificently dressed. All stop work. Boys
whisper to each other. Girls shake garments they are working upon
and grunt.*]

RAHAB—Hewers of wood and drawers of water!
    No Latin, Greek, or mathematics. None
    To wear the badge of haughty leadership.
    Hewers of wood and drawers of water!
    We men should organize for faith and prayer.
    Heaven is just. A little faith and prayer,
    And all the luxuries of earth are ours.
    (*To* DUDE.) Let us be gentlemen and serve the race
    As politicians.

DUDE—   That's the very thing.

RAHAB—'T will match our dignity.
DUDE—   And swell our purse.
GIRLS—Go, simpletons!
DUDE—   The girls would have us go.
BOYS—Go, simpletons!
DUDE—   The boys would have us go.
          Suppose we go ere trouble lends us speed.
FRONY—Say, man, why don't you go?
DUDE—   Explain and go.

[RAHAB *draws* DUDE *aside and whispers to him. Girl and boy go to them, look them over and write on pads. Boys and girls examine each other's work. Two girls smell a shoe and turn up their noses. Another girl holds up handkerchief she has made. Boy pretends to blow his nose and motions for it. Girl whips him over the head with it.* OLIVIA *takes horseshoe from* BLACKSMITH *and holds it up.* BLACKSMITH *hangs shoes on wall. Carpenter begins working-design on board. Shoemaker puts finishing touches on shoe. Girls measure each other for a dress. Two other girls take dirty, ragged little girl, who has entered, behind screen, and dress her in clothes taken from wall. Other girls sew on.*]

OLIVIA—(*Holds up horseshoe.*) This is well made. 'T is perfect, or
          near so.
BISHOP—How best define perfection?
OLIVIA—   , In this case
          'T is best done with a hammer.
BISHOP—   'T is the way.
OLIVIA—It is not Rahab's way.
BISHOP—   He counts for naught.
OLIVIA—The crowd he represents is troublesome.

[BLACKSMITH *has placed horseshoes on the wall so as to form the word " Work." He taps them gently with a piece of iron to attract attention.*]

BLACKSMITH—(*To* RAHAB.) Out! out!
GIRL—   Let's shake him out! [*Girls shake garments.*]
BOY AND GIRL—   Let's rhyme him out!
DUDE—Good sense dictates—
BLACKSMITH—   Good sense dictates.
RAHAB—   What? What?
DUDE—You see the people you've induced to leave
          For Africa.
OLIVIA—(*To* RAHAB.) They go and you remain?
RAHAB—They go, and I remain.
FRONY—   To live at ease
          On stolen fare.
DUDE—   They may come here, and then?
RAHAB—Let's go! [*They start.* FRONY, *girl and boy stand near the door and stop them.*]
TWO GIRLS— Let's go! [*They walk up against wall and look back.*]
          Rahab, a wall! Let's go!
BLACKSMITH—(*Raises hammer.*) A wall's a wall. I think he doesn't
          choose.

Re-enter WOMAN, *laughing.*

WOMAN—Such silly things! Rahab, they wait for you.
'T is pitiful to see such silly things.
They must be silly when a thing like you
Can make them sell their cotton and their mules.
What cloth you wear! What shoes! You roguish rogue!
Their hard-earned dollars weight your pockets now.
They will be here. Beware!

BLACKSMITH—(*To* RAHAB.)　　　　Suppose you go.

[*Girl and boy draw ugly picture of* RAHAB.]

FRONY—(*To* BOY *and* GIRL.) Now, draw him well. We want a
hearty laugh.

OLIVIA—They would be gentlemen and serve the race
As politicians.

BISHOP—　　　　Rahab, politics
Has been a game with you. Blindly you led.
As blindly were you followed.

RAHAB—　　　　　　　　I saw well.
If they did not, they have a chance to learn.

OLIVIA—They may learn yet. Think you it possible?

RAHAB—When did you bargain for the needed sense?

OLIVIA—Simplicity in them breeds theft in you.
A vote to them is life and death. You take
The vote and live. They give it you and die.

RAHAB—It is a game of sense. I play. They sleep.

OLIVIA—You love the race?

RAHAB—　　　　　I love the race? I lead.
Others may do the loving. I look up.

OLIVIA—I love Rahab. (*He turns toward her.*) I love Rahab.

RAHAB—　　　　　　　　　　　　　Woman,
That spurs me on to action.

OLIVIA—　　　　　　　That's your speech
Upon yourself. It spurs you on—

BISHOP—　　　　　　　　To death.

BLACKSMITH—Sharpen the spurs, Rahab.

FRONY—　　　　　　Rahab! [*He turns.*]

WOMAN—　　　　　　Rahab! [*He turns.*]

BLACKSMITH—Rahab, the Blacksmith gives you good advice.

FRONY—Rahab, we think of you as one would think
Of—of—

WOMAN—　　　This picture here. [*Girl shows picture. Boy is de-*
lighted. Girls throw sewing at RAHAB.]

A GIRL—　　　　　　O, we forgot.
Rahab, you did not earn the cloth you wear.
Thief! Thief!　　　　　[*Girls pick up sewing.*]

BLACHSMITH—　Thief! Thief!

WOMAN—　　　　　A silly thief!

FRONY—　　　　　　　A fool!

BLACKSMITH—(*Goes to* RAHAB.) My clothes are plain but paid for
    with my sweat. [*He rubs against* RAHAB, *who rubs off dirt
    with his hands.*]

FRONY—Be not so careful of your cloth, Rahab.

WOMAN—Your ruling passion will supply your need.

RAHAB—Ladies and gentlemen, a gentleman
    Like me—

DUDE—(*Straightens up and steps out.*) Like me!

RAHAB—(*To* DUDE.)   I am the orator!

DUDE—I am the gentleman.

RAHAB—   A gentleman
    Like me should have the treatment—

DUDE—   I should have.

RAHAB—Let us unite in this!

DUDE—   United we!
    I am the whole. Shadow me as I move. [*He moves about.*]

OLIVIA—A shadow asks a shadow to unite.
    A combination that combines two naughts!

[DUDE *goes to* RAHAB.]

DUDE—Are we two naughts?

RAHAB—   I am the orator.

DUDE—I am the other that will equal it.

RAHAB—Stand off a pace!

DUDE—   I fear!

RAHAB—   What fear you?

DUDE—   I
    Fear you—

RAHAB—   'T is spoken well.

DUDE—   Will play the fool
    And leave me out of it.

OLIVIA—   You wrangle well.
    Rahab, you are a leader?

RAHAB—   Yes!

DUDE—   Your name!
    My answer! Yes!

RAHAB —   Does this fine Dude disturb?
    [*All cry yes.*]
    Suppose we put him out. [*All cry no.*] Why not? He helps—

OLIVIA—To show what Rahab is.

BISHOP—   He is—

BLACKSMITH—(*Strikes anvil.*)   A sound!

[DUDE *stands beside* BLACKSMITH. *Girls put hands to ears as though to
listen.* FRONY *goes up to* RAHAB. *She puts hand to ear as though to
listen. She goes back to* WOMAN *and pretends to tell her something.*
WOMAN *plays same.* GIRL *and* BOY *play same and run to* BISHOP.
RAHAB *is alone. He turns around and seems lost.* BLACKSMITH
shouts as RAHAB *did in first act, and blows hard.*]

    I move me thus when I am glad at heart.

A GIRL—Who would I be?
BOY—   Myself!
WOMAN—   My own—
FRONY—   Sweet self!
[*All bow and retire to corners of room, leaving the* BISHOP, OLIVIA, *and*
RAHAB *in center of floor.* OLIVIA *opens her book—" The Negro and
His Hands."*]
                Now, find the laugh. Rahab might relish it.
RAHAB—Ladies and gentlemen, don't laugh at me.
        I might commit—
BISHOP—   You mean might suicide?
RAHAB—I might. The strain is hard. I might. Ladies,
        I might. Good gentlemen, I might. Don't laugh!
              [*All laugh save* BISHOP *and* OLIVIA.]
    BLACKSMITH—(*Striking shoe with hammer.*) Rahab, I liken this
        unto your brain.
    SHOEMAKER—(*Driving pegs into shoe.*) RAHAB, I liken pegs unto
        your teeth.   [*Works on at shoe.*]
    CARPENTER—(*Sawing board.*) Thus would I honor your smooth
        tongue, Rahab.   [*Carpenter planes a board.*]
FRONY—Let's laugh again.
OLIVIA—   No! no! I fear his tears.
BLACKSMITH—They might come rushing, rushing, Yes, they might.
RAHAB—(*Loudly.*) Ladies and gentlemen— [*Boys stop up ears with
        fingers. Girls stamp and hiss.*]
FRONY—(*Runs to* RAHAB.)   Do you not see
        They have no mind to listen? You are dull. [*Runs back.*]
RAHAB—(*To* DUDE.) Let us combine!
DUDE—   That is the word. Let us
        Combine—
RAHAB—   One friend! One friend!
DUDE—   To lesson you.
OLIVIA—Two fools at outs! One dulls the other's wits.
        Two scamps that dare not kiss the lip of Truth!
RAHAB—(*Looking around, baring his throat.*) Give me an instrument.
        The end must be!
        Give me an instrument! Life's cheating death!
              [*Boys hide tools.*]
BISHOP—There is no need of fear. Each give him one.
              [*All offer tools.*]
RAHAB—(*He motions them off.*) My misery may yet cream o'er my
        life.
WOMAN—I wonder if the Dude is seeking ends.
FRONY—Not to his nonsense, lying, trickery.
OLIVIA—Cowardly Dude, be brave awhile. Lesson
        Your friend in suicidal ends. Be quick!
              [*DUDE shakes his head.*]

BISHOP—(*Rises from chair.*) The Negro is no suicide as yet.
Some think it shows a most reserved strength.
It is a weakness. Mark my words and heed.
A race that is not suicidal has
Not wit enough—not pluck enough to rule.
WOMAN—Now, find the laugh. Rahab is Rahab still.
[OLIVIA *reads from her book.*]
OLIVIA—"There is a man who takes his daily fare
From such as know not life as life."
FRONY—(*Pointing to* RAHAB.) The man!
OLIVIA—"Who talks for votes and votes to suit his purse."
FRONY—The very man!
WOMAN— He stands the charges well.
RAHAB—Had you not me in mind in writing that?
OLIVIA—I had nothing in mind.
BISHOP— Are you the man?
FRONY—Let us not laugh. It grows too serious.
BISHOP—You are the man. You are the nothing. You—
The politician on whom politics
Casts witchery until your feet are set
In rapid motion. Peril follows then.
You have no light save that ambition lends,
And no man yet did ever walk by it
To a sure destiny. You have no thought
Save that which springs from trifling with itself.
You can not help a saucy whirlwind. Why?
You seldom know just when it will appear.
'T is here. 'T is there. 'T is spent in whirligigs.
If you approach it, woe unto your eyes.
'T is so with your poor thinking. Who can tell
When you indulge in moments serious?
Who ever saw you spend a silent hour
In linking what is now with what was then?
Thinking with you would be so out of place
That all your organism would rebel.
You might essay it for a moment, but
'T would be a moment filled with levity.
Offer a helping hand? No man of sense
Would so transgress. 'T is very dangerous.
A leader you? Laugh at yourself and quit.
OLIVIA—A little laugh would so improve his face.
BISHOP—A leader, you?
OLIVIA— Do ask that tenderly.
He has a past he fain would bolster up.
BISHOP—(*Tenderly.*) A leader you?
RAHAB— Who says that I am not?

[DUDE *stands behind* BLACKSMITH *and views him disgustingly. Boy and
girl stand behind the* BISHOP *and applaud him gently.* FRONY *and*
WOMAN *hold book and seem to read as* BISHOP *talks. Girls stand*

together and rock to and fro, holding work in hands. Boys hold tools
ready for work. OLIVIA *pats them on heads. The* BISHOP *holds*
string attached to a dirtg bottle.]

BISHOP—The conjurer of anti-bellum days
          Would bottle up a few indifferent herbs,
          Mixed with a little sugar, salt, and oil.
          He called the bottle Jack. A foot of string
          Attached it to his hand. He swayed and groaned.
             [*Boys, girls, and women sway and groan.*]
          He kissed it, patted it, and spoke to it.
       [*Boys, girls, and women so treat things in their hands.*]
          "Now, are you ready, Jack? Let's see! Let's see!"
                   [*They examine things and nod.*]
          "Let us begin. I start. You follow, Jack.
             [*They begin to swing things in their hands.*]
          Now, this way! That way! Any way you please!
                 [*They swing in keeping with words.*]
          You swung your way and thereby told the truth.
          Let all who are in doubt or love or fear
          Consult with you, good Jack, and fortune fate."
OLIVIA—Rahab, consult with Jack and fortune fate.
BISHOP—You are as simple as that conjurer.
          You hold a vote is ample remedy
          For all the ills a backward race may have.
          You say: "My people, vote your sentiments.
          Be sure they are not yours. You must not think
          Of things political. It spoils the drift
          Of ancient teachings. Vote your sentiments
          The while you taste the drink that buys the vote.
          Your sentiments are good as gold. Therefore,
          Be certain that you get a fair exchange.
          Neglect your work to foster sentiments.
          Neglect your family to cast a vote.
          Be sure the man who feeds and shelters you
          Shall feel the weight of all your sentiments
          Advancing his opponent. Simply vote,
          And you are great beyond all measurement.
          Naught else can equal voting. Simply vote,
          And all the past is as it had not been.
          Voting is magical. The present holds
          No paradise this key can not unlock!"
OLIVIA—A leader you?
RAHAB—   Who says—
OLIVIA—   The Bishop says—
BISHOP—Your votes and follies are an equal twain.
          A leader you?
RAHAB—   Who—?
DUDE—(*To* RAHAB.)   Save your breath.
RAHAB—   I will.

OLIVIA—Observe your thumb and finger. [*He looks at them.*] Make
them fit
Your nose.
FRONY— 'T will save your breath. A book! Observe!
[*She holds book before him. He folds his arms and looks at ceiling.*]
WOMAN—Observe the men that I bring back with me. [*Exit quickly.*]
BISHOP—Observe the worth of manhood's simple ways.
Observe your carelessness and root it out.
Observe your roughness and the cure for it.
Observe your ignorance and wisdom it.
Observe your savagery—
Enter old man and followers, men and women, whom RAHAB *is about to
send to Africa.*
OLD MAN— To savage parts
We soon set sail. Rahab, we wait on you.
[RAHAB *moves among them and bows.*]
Re-enter WOMAN *with two officers.*
OFFICER—Rahab, we wait on you. [*They lead him out.*]
FRONY— What of the Dude?
DUDE—I am converted.
BLACKSMITH— Take a hammer then. [*He takes one.*]
DUDE—I feel like growing eloquent.
OLIVIA— Proceed
Upon the basis of the anvil there.
OLD MAN—Our leader's gone.
BISHOP— To pay for robbing you.
OLD MAN—The proof?
BISHOP There's proof enough. His clothes are part.
Re-enter OFFICER *with beaver hat, coat, and vest.*
OFFICER—The rest we will secure when he's in jail.
DUDE—Secure what I have on when I'm in jail.
[OFFICER *leads* DUDE *out.*]
OLD MAN—(*To followers.*) Let's try again. We must to Africa.
WOMEN FOLLOWERS—We must.
[*Little American flags are passed to members of school.*]
OLD MAN— That is our home.
MEN FOLLOWERS— Our home!
WOMEN FOLLOWERS— Our home!
OLD MAN—"My Country 'T is of Thee" I can not sing.
[*The* BLACKSMITH *sings the three first lines of hymn.* BISHOP, OLIVIA,
and rest of school wave flags.]
OLD MAN—Hush! hush! It means not anything to me.
MEN FOLLOWERS—Not anything!
WOMEN FOLLOWERS— Not anything.
ALL— Nothing.
OLD MAN—What have we given to this goodly land?
BISHOP—A little muscle and a world of sighs.
OLD MAN—We won no victories on bloody fields?
BISHOP—Full many, and we have their heritage.

OLD MAN—Their heritage! A little space to breathe—
 A fruitless hour to feel one's loneliness—
 A country that is one ignoble grave.
BISHOP—Old Man, you wrong the land in which we dwell.
 As you have said it is a goodly land.
 The race is not the unit. It is man.
 The individual eclipses all.
 Who rules his fireside with kindly tact,
 Who robs his neighborhood of ancient sloth,
 Will have no fruitless hour, no loneliness.
[OLIVIA *offers flags to* OLD MAN *and followers. They refuse them.*]
BISHOP—Ignoble graves but hide ignoble dead.
OLD MAN—(*Points to flag in* BISHOP'S *hand.*) Ignoble you to touch
 so foul a rag.
 It flaunts a lie in Heaven's trustful face.
 You would be loyal? Negro loyalty
 Is paid in shot and flame. Disloyal we!
  [*Followers move about and bow assent.*]
 Be wise! Join us! Kindle our hated race!
 To Africa! To Africa with them!
 Expansion may expand to Uncle Sam's
 Discomfiture. Our moment then! Be wise!
 A foreign foe may ask our sturdy arm.
 Our moment then! We'll strike! We'll strike! We'll
 strike!
 Be wise! Kindle the race! A man? Lead on!
  [BISHOP, OLIVIA, *and school wave flags.*]
BISHOP—Disloyal to my native land?
 A traitor to the stripes and stars?
 I lift this tried and sturdy hand
 To forge my brother's prison bars?
  Perish the hellish thought!
 My all shall go as a true patriot's ought.
 [*Followers of* OLD MAN *shake baggage at* BISHOP.]
 Justice at times may slightly swerve
 And turn the course of freedom back.
 Her blinded presence tend to nerve
 The mob that puts me to the rack,
  Yet I am what I am—
 A force to guard the rights of Uncle Sam.
[*Followers start to rush out. Pupils wave flags and start to follow.*
 OLD MAN *beckons, and followers return. Pupils wave flags and
resume places.*]
 My faith looks up through blood and tears,
  And tarries at the golden dawn
 Whose beams slant out across the years
  Proclaiming Freedom fully born.
  I must do what I can
 To hasten on this boon to struggling man.

[*Followers yell no, no. Pupils cry yes, yes.* OLD MAN *starts to go out but stops.*]
BISHOP—(*Pointing to* OLD MAN.) He who complains is but a laggard born,
    A simpleton, a coward. Mark him well!
    He prays of his complaints, and straight complains
    Him of his prayers. To him all lands are hells.
[OLD MAN *starts to rush out.* BLACKSMITH *dances before him and stops him.*]
BLACKSMITH—Abrupt your course! List to a random thought!
    Stir up a dust somehow! Squeeze out a sigh!
    Bethink you of some trick to murder peace!
    Pass on! Pass on! Your mood is moody still!
                          [*Exit* OLD MAN.]
[*Followers start to rush out, but return when the* BISHOP *speaks.*]
BISHOP—Why chafe you so, my brothers, O, my brothers?
    Why strain you ever at a weight you bear not?
    Why cloak yourselves against occasion's breezes
    That waft to you the perfumes whose inhaling
    Divorces Truth from her false cousin, Fancy?
    Why form a helmet 'gainst some dreamy evil
    That blinds you ever-madly, madly blinds you?
    Why gather troubles chance has left around you
    As one would gather pebbles by the wayside?
    Why with these airy troubles storm the Present
    That bird-like comes singing your sure redemption?
    Why of these airy troubles raise a bulwark
    That severs you from God and God's anointed?
        [*They draw nearer and strain to hear.*]
    Know you the eye that makes a mark of vengeance
    Fathers a soul warped by its degradation?
    Know you the soul that ever glows and triumphs
    Must harbor naught of malice or of envy?
    My brothers, O, my brothers, be not wanting
    In the clear vision that has led the nations
    From life barbaric unto life whose oneness
    Proves, as naught else can prove, God's hand in nature.
    There is a chance. It lies in the discretion
    That hails no spectre-past to thwart the present,
    That slays no happy future for the slaying.
    There is a chance. It springs from out the wedding
    Of native thought to universal triumph.
    Too hard you say? Think you a world is conquered
    By blowing bubbles on a bed of lilies?
        [*They back out slowly in a body.*]
    The wine of life is brewing, O, my brothers!
    The hand of God upholds and tilts the chalice.
    Quaff quickly, brothers, quaff! You won't? Your failing
    Deserves the wrath of God, the scourge of nations.

Their cudgel, use-inured and anger-pointed,
Is all-sufficient in the day of trial.
Beware its stroke, my brothers, O, my brothers!
[*They disappear as last words are uttered. Pupils wave flags, approach*
BISHOP, *bow and retire.*]
(*To Pupils.*)—Let us be true to worship, trained in toil,
A standing menace to what gives offense,
And this our land shall be our paradise.
Know you, my faithful children, that the man
Of toil best honored is. His sweaty brow
Is his well-done in life, his grace in death.
The cross and handicrafts are God and man
Revealing each to each. Remember that!
[*All bow assent. Enter girl from behind screen, holding dirty, ragged
clothes in hand.*]
GIRL—I am so clean! I feel so good! Thanks! thanks!
Look at my clothes! They fit! They fit! They fit!
Such darling girls you are! Thanks! thanks? thanks! thanks!
[*Girl moves about while talking. Pupils move and wave flags..*]
BISHOP—Work is the basis of life's heritage.
It is the mountain, bottoming at sea,
And rising far above the angry waves
Whereon a people's hopes may fruit in life.
It is the slayer of full many boasts,
The wiper-out of dream-encompassed ends.
The Negro of the past had faith in faith.
Henceforward he must rise to faith in sight.
He visions what is clearly tangible,
And tangles visions with reality.
He needs the wisdom that is won of toil,
The patience that is bred of constant aim,
The hopefulness that stales not out of use,
A sense of worth that slays all else but worth,
A view of God that lets God regulate
Life's devious ways without the prayers of fools.
Work is the basis of life's heritage.
ALL—Thanks! thanks! thanks! thanks! thanks! thanks!
[*Wave flags.*]
BISHOP—(*Looking up.*) Thanks, Master, thanks!
Curtain.

ACT IV.

SCENE I.—A Narrow Street.

[*Enter* NOAH *slowly, stroking his beard. The* BISHOP *and* FRONY *follow him at a distance.*]

FRONY—Noah! [*He looks back and grunts.*]

BISHOP—Noah! [*He looks back, clears his throat and goes out.* FRONY *follows him.*] A man of few words and much beard! May be unpleasant dreams of his beard have added to his melancholly. 'T is often so reported. Such a beard costs fifty years of toil, tears, and expectations. It is worth, in this case, all but the life of the owner. He might exchange it for the undoing of Caleb. The end! The ungodly end! Caleb has disappeared. Now, Olivia goes. The ungodly end! No! no! Be thwarted, logic! I would have no image of that end. [*Reenter* FRONY.] The report, Frony?

FRONY—It is true. Caleb went weighted with baggage.

BISHOP—What of Olivia?

FRONY—She comes this way, baggage in hand and good-by on lip.

BISHOP—Has Noah found tongue?

FRONY—No!

BISHOP—He may.

FRONY—When he loses his beard.

BISHOP—Or Caleb finds his reward.

    Enter OLIVIA, *baggage in hand, followed by* NOAH.

OLIVIA—Caleb shall soon find his reward.

ALL—Olivia!

OLIVIA—Good-by!

FRONY—(*Removing* OLIVIA'S *hat.*) Good-by!

BISHOP—(*Taking baggage.*) Good-by!

NOAH—Say good-by for me.

BISHOP AND FRONY—Good-by!

OLIVIA—This is a serious company.

NOAH—Yes! Say good-by for me.

BISHOP AND FRONY—Good-by!

OLIVIA—This is a misguided company.

BISHOP—"Caleb's the man! Caleb's secure. Caleb shall soon find his reward!" These are your speeches.

OLIVIA—Yes! As Frony says: "Woman's wit may cudgel man's." Caleb's the man for what? He's secure in what? His reward shall be what?

BISHOP—I might have questioned thus.

FRONY—(*Going to* BISHOP.) Yes! Why did you not?

OLIVIA—He is the man to expiate his crimes. He is secure in the coils of retribution. His reward shall be death.

NOAH—Death!

FRONY—(*To* OLIVIA, *patting her on shoulder.*) We make progress.

BISHOP—Why this suspense?

OLIVIA—Why your charge? Your speeches are: "Reflect, my child! You should not wed this hell-builder upon earth. Your steps are led not heavenward. My daughter is in love. She needs no father." You charged—

FRONY—On and on!

OLIVIA—I balanced it with suspense.

NOAH—Caleb! Suspense! Death! [*Looks at beard in pocket-book.*]

OLIVIA—Good nature writhes under such charges. Sharpened wits though are the remedy.

FRONY—Your answer, Bishop?

BISHOP—You saw! You heard! You know!

NOAH—No, not what I know.

BISHOP—You were so kind—

OLIVIA—To Caleb?

BISHOP—Yes!

OLIVIA—I was kind to Patsy.

BISHOP—There was I misled.

NOAH—There was I—but death!

OLIVIA—Our school first lived in Patsy's mind. I came with views unsuited to our people. She was my teacher. I built upon her thought. Now, see the result. Her wish was I speak well of Caleb until her taking off. I did so. You misjudged.

BISHOP—My child, Caleb asked me for your hand.

[NOAH *is greatly agitated.*]

OLIVIA—Perchance he heard how you charged. He then counter-charged for fun in his fiendish way.

NOAH—Fiendish? Yes, fiendish! Death!

OLIVIA—You remember how he ran when I appeared?

BISHOP—Yes!

OLIVIA—You remember my ideal man?

BISHOP—Yes!

OLIVIA—What more was needed?

BISHOP—Yes! yes! But your speeches were— Well— Your pardon—your pardon! [*He embraces and kisses her.*]

FRONY—Bishop! [*He turns her loose.* FRONY *embraces her.*] A part of her pardon's mine.

NOAH—Take my pardon, too. [BISHOP *and* FRONY *embrace her.*]

BISHOP—What of Caleb's reward?

NOAH—Death!

OLIVIA—In a sane hour his conscience mastered him.

NOAH—Conscience! [*Shakes his head.*]

OLIVIA—He went to yon lone wood with a piece of meat, a jug of water, and a dagger.

FRONY—(*Aside.*) Ah, the baggage!

OLIVIA—The meat and water come first. Then comes the dagger.

NOAH—Quickly! Surely!

BISHOP—Poor lad!

NOAH—What said you, Bishop?
OLIVIA—Poor crazed lad!
NOAH—Sympathy misplaced is hope hopeless.
BISHOP—He was crazed, you say?   How?
OLIVIA—Drink! Cocaine! Cigarettes!
BISHOP—(*To* NOAH.)   Can you forgive?
NOAH—Can I forget my loss, my beard?
BISHOP—(*Aside*.)   I think not!
OLIVIA—Your loss, father?   You did not explain it.
NOAH—Explain it?   No!
FRONY—Hereafter let us exchange wedding mysteries for bearded
ones.
OLIVIA—Must I be off to Boston without hat or baggage?
FRONY—To Boston?
BISHOP—To Boston?
OLIVIA—I go to speak for the school.
    [NOAH *grunts and breathes in a way that shows he is relieved.*]
BISHOP—(*Gives her baggage.*)   Good-by!   My prayers are yours.
FRONY—(*Puts on hat.*)   Good-by!   I'll to the train with you.
OLIVIA—Good-by!   Good-by, father!
NOAH—Good-by!   Woo business!   [*Exeunt* OLIVIA *and* FRONY.]
BISHOP—Noah, can you—?
NOAH—Forgive?   No!   [*Exit looking at beard.*]
BISHOP—Woman's wit did cudgel man's.   Her speeches!   My witless-
ness!   'Twas fair enough!   I should have known.   Poor crazed lad!
Rahab is responsible.   Well, I have no beard to mourn and revenge, and
I may render the poor lad service.   I will search him out.   [*Exit.*]
    The curtain rises on next scene immediately.

SCENE II—A Wood.   Before Caleb's Hut.

[*At the rising of the curtain* CALEB *is seated on a rock with his back to
the hut.   He looks 'like a wild man.   His hair is unkept.   He is
nigh shirtless.   His legs are bare from knees down.   They have been
broken by a fall, and are bloody from the attack of a dog.   It is a
dreary wood.   A piece of meat hangs from a tree.   A jug of water
hangs from roof of hut.   The moon and stars give light.   He hugs his
legs, looks from side to side, pants and lolls his tongue like a dog.*]

CALEB—My legs!   My legs!   [*Points to meat.*]   Meat!   [*To drink.*]
        Drink!
    This—this means death.
    Three days, three days and nights, I've suffered thus.
    In putting up that meat I fell.   My legs
    Were broken.   I crawled here.   I here remain.
    A stray dog found me here.   [*Points to sores.*]   Here! here!
        here! here!
    He bit me, tore my flesh.   Here! here! here! here!
    He left no flesh upon the bones.   Here! here—!

My legs! My legs! Death woos! I fear? No! no!
[*He tries to rise, but falls back.*]
I must, therefore I will. My dagger's keen!
[*Holds it up.*]
I have not strength of heart to use it yet.
If I could sleep a little, I might wake
With strength enough—enough. I 'll try! My legs!
[*He tries to sleep. He pants and lolls his tongue.*]
Enter BISHOP *aud* DOCTOR *unseen.*
BISHOP—(*To* DOCTOR.) That 's Caleb—
DOCTOR—   The degenerate?
BISHOP—   Yes! yes!
CALEB—(*Faintly.*) My legs! My legs!
DOCTOR—   He is a parricide?
BISHOP—That drove him here—
CALEB—(*Very faintly.*)   My legs! My legs!
BISHOP—   To die.
       A little daily.
DOCTOR—   Why his many crimes?
BISHOP—He claims his mother sinned ere he was born.
       This tainted him. Therefore his wicked course.
CALEB—I can't! Off, sleep! My legs! My legs! Meat! Drink!
       [*Takes up dagger and kisses it.*]
       ˙ꞯy only friend! I kiss you! Oh! My legs!
       ꞇ ꞁe sinned ere I was born. Therefore I am
       My present self. She sinned! I am—! My legs!
       [*He tries to grasp dagger tightly.*]
       Have I the strength? Have I the heart? I 'll try!
       [*He trembles. His teeth chatter.*]
       I 'm cold! I 'm hot! I 'm sad! I 'm woe-begone!
       I have a mind that puts me out of mind.
       The stars shall set, shall set and rise, and I—
       Be true, good blade—shall be as cold as they.
BISHOP—Your heard?
DOCTOR—   His mother sinned! A dog's excuse!
BISHOP—Pure mother-love, consoling mother-love
       Is the one balm that long-lost Eden gave
       To guilty man and could not take away.
       By mother-love man is whate'er he is.
       For mother-love he struggles, conquers, dies.
       Through mother-love the stars his kindred are.
       Shall anything that evil man calls guilt
       Dry up this love within the breast of him
       Whose bone, whose sinue, and whose blood are hers?
       No! No! She did not sin. She loved! She loved!
       Are we not taught love is the law fulfilled?
CALEB—O, God, if I have sinned because the blood
       Thou gavest me was tainted ere my birth,

Whose is the wrong? Whose is the reckoning?
Master, I leave it all with Thee—with Thee.
Men sneer and say: ''Be guided by your will!''
I have no will! I never had a will!
Thy fate, O God, did rob me of my will!
BISHOP—A babe was he whose soft and dimpled cheeks
Invited kisses from a seraph's lips.
A gentle mother thought his coo a prayer.
Old seers beheld in him God's messenger.
But he through Rahab sank and sank and sank,
And cheers him with the thought—God made him so.
CALEB—The stars shall set, shall set and rise, and I—
Begin, good blade—shall be as cold as they.

[*He tries to stab himself. They take dagger from him. He does not
recognize them. He hugs his legs more tightly and snaps at them
dog-fashion. They examine his legs.*]

DOCTOR—His legs are broken.
BISHOP—   Oh, what savage bites!
The flesh is gone! The bones stare out at us!
DOCTOR—They must be taken off. The hospital—
BISHOP—That's death! That's death?
CALEB—   My legs! My legs! The morgue!
The morgue! I see! How cold it is! My legs!
Gentlemen, are you gentlemen? My legs!
BISHOP—His mind! It wavers now.
DOCTOR—   'T s better so.
Its weakness is far stronger than its strength.
CALEB—I'm at the hospital! You've cut them off!
You brutes cut off my legs! Off! off! I say!
I see! They're coming back! Come on, good legs!
Off! Off! You butchers, off! Your knives are sharp!
Come on, good legs, and take me from the morgue.
Off! off! you brutes! You'd butcher me again!
Come, my right leg! Come, my left leg! That's it!
On, good right leg? On, good left leg? [*He feels.*] Yes! Yes!
Welcome, tried friends! Let's from this cursed place!
Back! back! you brutes! Your knives are sharp. Back!
  Back!
Let's down the steps! Back! back! you brutes! Right on!
Down—down the steps! Now, we are half-way down.
My right foot, you shall not, shall not turn round.
'T is done! The toes are where the heel should be.
I now go up a step and down a step.
Back! back! you brutes! Your knives! Your knives! My legs!
My right leg's off and hops up, step by step.
My left leg's off and hops down, step by step.
My body falls! You'll take it to the morgue.
The morgue's so cold—so cold—so— What—is—this? [*Falls.*]

DOCTOR—(*Looks at him.*) 'T is death! [*He walks off.* BISHOP *looks
down on him.*] His mother sinned ere he was born.
    This tainted him, therefore his wicked course.
BISHOP—No! no! She did not sin. Caleb was led
    To that belief.
DOCTOR—   Was led?
BISHOP—   Rahab's the man.
DOCTOR—Rahab? His sin is great. I would know all.
BISHOP—His evil genius wrought this ruin here.
DOCTOR—Eternal vengeance should pursue him then.
BISHOP—It does pursue. Perhaps his spirit now
    Is mingling with— [*He hesitates.*]
DOCTOR—   The damned! A spade's a spade.
BISHOP—I know the man, his life. But yesterday
    He did confess to me. Noah was there.
    His gloomy cell and gloomier deeds are weights
    He can not bear. He takes no food, no drink.
DOCTOR—How wrought he such a ruin?
BISHOP—   Rahab's speech
    Charmed Caleb when a youth.
DOCTOR—   Many were charmed.
BISHOP—Then followed teachings that few youths could stand.
    His love for parents dwindled day by day.
    Restraint was not for him who knew so much.
    He hated work and all who favored it.
    His ideal gentleman must ever eat
    The bread another earns and wear the clothes
    He picks up, borrows, steals. He hated God
    Because he saw his fellows prosperous.
DOCTOR—This came from Rahab's teaching?
BISHOP—   All of it.
    A living lesson eats into the soul.
DOCTOR—Caleb's belief was strong. How was it shaped?
BISHOP—When he was thwarted of some luxury
    Rahab would say: "This is your mother's sin."
    And quote the text that seems to bear it out.
DOCTOR—I wonder if he's dead.
BISHOP—   Who's dead?
DOCTOR—   Rahab!
BISHOP—Noah is with him. He will bring us word.
DOCTOR—Rahab was satisfied?
BISHOP—   Are devils?
DOCTOR—   No!
BISHOP—Caleb must drink, become a bondless slave
    To cigarettes.
DOCTOR—   Noah delays—delays.
BISHOP—While Caleb slept Rahab would hold cocaine
    So that he'd sniff it as he breathed.
DOCTOR—   The end

Was then in sight. [*Aside.*] Noah, report the end.

BISHOP—This ruin here was not responsible.

DOCTOR—Rahab thinks what? Or what thought he? Past tense
    For him.

BISHOP—   Past tense? Ah, yes! "Fool, fool was I.
    O, pardon Caleb, God. I should be damned."

DOCTOR—He so confessed?

BISHOP—   He did.

Enter NOAH, *hurriedly.*

DOCTOR—(*To* NOAH.)   He is—? Let's hear!

NOAH—Dead! Dead!

BISHOP—   His last words were—?

NOAH—   "Fool, fool was I.
    O, pardon Caleb, God. I should be damned."
                    [*He sees* CALEB.]
    Dead? [*He kneels by him.*] I'll forgive. God help me to
    forgive.

DOCTOR—Man is a mystery.

BISHOP—   He started pure.
    But now? What of the best man now? Virtue
    In some mysterious way has mothered sin.
    Evil may back-step till it ends in good.

DOCTOR—The proverb saith: "We have all been born,
    But not interred." The thought's worth thinking on.

BISHOP—Another saith: "Man is like the grass."

[DOCTOR *puts his arm around* BISHOP *and looks at* CALEB. NOAH
    remains kneeling.]

Curtain. It rises on next scene as quickly as possible.

SCENE III.—Grounds of Industrial School.

[*On the rising of the curtain* NOAH *is embracing and kissing* OLIVIA, *who
holds bank-checks in her hand. The* BISHOP *and* FRONY *stand apart
and point to them. Boys and girls of the Industrial School eye* DUDE,
*who is now United States' soldier. He is so uniformed. He stands
erect in rear and holds large flag. Old man and followers look up at
flag and wave little flags. Girls and boys wave flags.*]

NOAH—My Olivia was right.

OLIVIA—Thanks!

BISHOP—My Olivia will ever be right.

OLIVIA—Thanks!

NOAH—My Olivia—

BISHOP—My Olivia—

OLIVIA—A daughter's thanks to both!

FRONY—Out with your checks, Olivia! A hundred thousand, did
you say?

OLIVIA—Yes! More is to follow.

FRONY—Thanks to the givers!

DUDE—Thanks! Let's use the gifts. More grounds, workshops, dormitories.

OLD MAN—Thanks, Olivia!

FOLLOWERS—Yes, thanks!

BISHOP—You did it all yourself?

NOAH—Is she not Olivia?

OLD MAN—Have faith in Olivia.

FOLLOWERS—Do!

BLACKSMITH—(*To* FOLLOWERS.) How changed you are!

DUDE—And I?

GIRLS—(*Pointing to* DUDE.) The Dude!

DUDE—(*Indignantly.*) No! The soldier.

FRONY—(*Goes to* DUDE.) Your clothes have a brave front.

[GIRLS *approach* DUDE, *clap hands and retire.*]

BLACKSMITH—(*To* DUDE.) They may applaud you next.

BISHOP—(*To* OLIVIA.) Give us the story of your enterprise.

OLIVIA—Chance threw me with a group of millionaires.
    I doubted, fretted, feared. At last I spoke.
    The speech was short and simple. See the checks!

BISHOP—They lost no time in writing them?

OLIVIA—   A tale
    Our folks oft slumber o'er drew tears from them.

FRONY—And they left checks with you.

OLD MAN—   The difference!

DUDE—'T is plainly seen.

OLD MAN—   Appreciation sends
    A hundred thousand us-ward. Therefore we
    Should have—

BISHOP—   Ten million bank accounts.

OLD MAN—   Yes! yes!
    We have appreciation now.

FOLLOWERS—   We have.

BISHOP—Greatness holds trust with you, Olivia.
    Your stock in trade? Grit, health, and breathing space.
    Your spirit mutinies 'gainst time and tide.
    You see no inch that may not make an ell.
    You woo no aim you do not wed in time.

NOAH—Why do you pause? True words and precious words
    Are these you speak. Why do you pause, I say?
    Speak on! Pause not!

OLD MAN—   Now pause he must; for time
    And praise entrap her not.

NOAH—(*Stroking his beard.*) Good! Good! 'T is true!

FRONY—You speak like men. Redeem a faulty past.

[GIRLS *embrace and kiss* OLIVIA.]

BLACKSMITH—A woman's way!
FRONY— 'T is more sincere than speech.
  Redeem a faulty past.
BLACKSMITH—(*To men.*) Suppose we do.
  [*Men start to* OLIVIA.]
OLIVIA—Good sirs, I need a rest. [*They stop.*]
FRONY—(*Kisses her.*) She needs a rest.
  [FOLLOWERS *laugh and pat each other.*]
OLD MAN—(*To* FOLLOWERS.) Redeem the past we must.
FOLLOWERS— We must.
DUDE— We must.
BISHOP—The change was sudden.
OLD MAN— And sincere.
BISHOP— The cause?
OLD MAN—Your speech did warn.
BISHOP— What then?
OLD MAN— We found Rahab
  An evil influence.
DUDE— His death paid not
  The havoc that he wrought.
  [FOLLOWERS *move about and look at their ragged clothes.*]
OLD MAN—(*Pointing to* FOLLOWERS.) Behold his work!
  The homes he ruined shall condemn him here.
NOAH—The soul he ruined shall condemn him there.
OLD MAN—Henceforth we labor with Olivia.
  [OLIVIA *bows.* FOLLOWERS *bow.*]
BISHOP—(*To* DUDE.) You look the man that's needed in the wars.
DUDE—I will remember me to be a man.
[*Boy holds flag.* GIRLS *turn* DUDE *around and examine his clothes.*]
BISHOP—Let each remember him to be a man.
  Who is down-trodden? He who thorns his course.
  Who is a weakling? He who weds with sloth.
  Who fails ignobly? He who cultivates
  The aims that grovel and the wits that shame.
  Let each remember him to be a man;
  And, brothers mine, the world has naught to give
  That may not nestle in your willing hands.
OLD MAN—I like that speech, my brother. Speak right on!
FOLLOWERS—Right on!
DUDE— Right on!
BISHOP— What say you girls?
GIRLS— Right on!
OLIVIA—Right on to work! 'T is well enough to stir
  One's blood with talk. 'T is better still to make
  That talk a text and work the sermon out.
  I go to work. [*Exit quickly.*]
OLD MAN— We go to work. [*Exit* OLD MAN *with* FOLLOWERS.]
BLACKSMITH— To work!

[BLACKSMITH, *boys, and girls run out.*]

DUDE—I go to war.   Some say the Negro shirks
The tasks of peace.   Who says he will not fight?
I go to war.   [*Exit, bearing flag with dignity.*]

[FRONY *starts to run after* DUDE.   BISHOP *and* NOAH *stop her.*]

BISHOP—(*To* FRONY.)   To war?

FRONY—(*After freeing herself.*)   To work.   [*Exit quickly.*]

NOAH—(*Verg solemnly.*)   At last!
Your words!   My beard!   Olivia's success!
At last!   [*Exit slowly.*]

BISHOP—   How safe and handy is plain truth!
My words!   His beard!   Olivia's success!
Hers is success.   Failure?   'T is a misfit.
To coincide is life.   One measures not
His native force.   He sees no chains that bind
His ready out-put to a waiting need.
He tries.   He fails.   He tries and fails again.
Each trial curbs him in the onward race.
Each failure veers him from a happy goal.
"Upon such terms," says he, "life is not life.
False Life and I are dwelling by a stream.
I thirst.   Life tosses water on the shore.
The shore is sand, and I am thirsty still.
Away, false Life, away!   I'll drink!   I'll lave
My thirsty limbs!   I've drunk!   Where is the ground?
My limbs are awkward.   They belong on shore.
They splash!   My mouth!   My nose!   My ears!   I sink!
My head is up!   False legs!   False arms!   I sink!
Up once again!   I—choke!   I—I—I—sink!"
Failure?   'T is a misfit.   Success is what?
'T is measurement of self.   'T is measurement
Of all the forces that encounter self.
'T is fitting these together day by day.
'T is seeing goals with eyes that never blink.
'T is finding desert spots and changing them
So that their fruitage stars man's ancient lot,
And links his freedom with the linked spheres.   [*Exit.*]

Curtain.   End.